DESTRUCTION
OF
MAN

ABRAHAM SMITH

TMB·024

1. Breakdown Time (3:00)
2. Bleed That Line (2:32)

DESTRUCTION
OF
MAN

ABRAHAM
SMITH

For music and more information:
http://thirdmanbooks.com/destructionofman
password: buckhorn

Destruction of Man. Copyright © 2018 by Abraham Smith.

For information:
Third Man Books, LLC, 623 7th Ave S, Nashville, Tennessee 37203.

Printed in Nashville, Tennessee.

A CIP record is on file with the Library of Congress.

FIRST EDITION

All photos taken by Abraham Smith
Book cover and layout design by Tristan McNatt
Edited by Kimberly Baugh

"Bleed that Line" and "Breakdown Time"
Recorded by Jacob Thompson
Druid City Time and Space Ship Studios
Vocal: Abraham Smith
Accordion: Emily Ondine Wittman
Drums: Craig Pickering

ISBN 978-0-9974578-1-0

FOR

EDWARD MEISEGEIER

&

WILLIAM PFALZGRAF

EPIGRAPH

BASIL BUNTING

CONTENTS

I: TRACTOR BLISTER SONG MOUTH HAWK VULTURE SONG DIESEL BEAUTY MICE SONG DESTRUCTION SONG MY TRY AT WAYS IN II

II: STRING THEORY BABBLE PERSONAL CHICKEN MAIM WEASEL BODY MIND BUTTONS THEIR FATE VOLITION THE SEA THE SEA MAPLE NONFICTION MULL COYOTE NO MONEY FOR DUMP FEES TEETH MORN LAND FARMS YOU RAT X

III: ARMY SEEING FIRING ROCKPICK ROCKPILE COUNTRY SILENCE BEARS BACKS TRICKY CLICKY STUCK PROPHESY MAIM SADNESS METAL MONEY WAR BIRD LUST SUDDEN ONE RAG GASCAN RED TIP RED DEEP AND SO MUCH MORE YOU CAN KISS GOODBYE XXII

IV: MORE MONEY MEDITATION SOME HYPOTHETICALS FECUNDITY CALL ME IF YOU HAVE GREEN EATS WHAT LASTS MOUTHS OR TOES THE HISTORY OF KLEENEX AGAIN THE RURAIL NOSE OUTOFDOORS THE FUTURE THE PAST DINING SUFFERING POKING AT GREEN EATS WITH A PISSIN REED XXXVI

V: CROWS FOR PETS ANCESTOR SEXUAL RELATE SHUN MORE HAWK OBSCURE VAPE SHUN MORE BUZZARD BOD BLUES COLLUSION WOODTICKS GEESE ICE GAS SIPHONING TRACTOR CUT METAL WITH SOMETHING NOT MEANT TO CUT METAL WITH WHEN EVERYTHING IS BROKEN NOSTALGIA THE MANGER THE MANGE AMATEUR METALLURGY MOSQUITO XLVI

VI: BUCKHORN TEETHTASTING ON THE PASSAGE OF THYME CHEESE ORPHAN SPACKLE TURTLES TIGHT TURNS DIESEL WILL NEVER SEE THE DOOR CAN TASTE IT EVEN NOW AND IT'S BEEN 11 HOURS TRACTORS SEEDS DEBTS SEXINESS THE INVENTION OF THE WHEEL IS TIED UP UMBILICALLY LVIII

VII: A MEMORY NEVER YOU HAD IT MAKES LOVE OF THE .... **LXX**
BODY OF THE SKIDSTEER OF THE CARCASS OF THE
SOFTNESS THE HARDNESS OF HER LEG OF A TRAIN
OF BUILDING THINGS OF DANCERS OF VARIOUS
KINDS WITH SOME NOTES ON FORGETFULNESS
MORE PECKS AT LOVE AND CUTTING UP A DEER IS
A CRAZE DOGS DANCE AROUND THE DANGLE THE
DANG HOLE VARIOUS AND HUNGRY

VIII: CHEMICAL HELL MONEY AXES THE HISTORY OF .... **LXXVIII**
PEOPLE PENNY PINCHERS THE HISTORY OF BAD
BACKS AND A STEPBYSTEP DESCRIPTION OF HOW
TO CURE THEM FEET OR OX STRONG MEN

IX: AGRARIAN CONTROL ISSUE DEERFLY HORSEFLY .... **LXXXVI**
HIVES GOTTEN THEREBY THE TALE OF THE ASSPINCH
GOOSE THE TALE OF PISSED TATER MUTSCH

X: LOST TEETH MORE SOME POSSIBILITES IDENTITY .... **XCIV**
PLACE IN TIME AND WHAT A PASTORAL PILE OF SHIT
COUNTRY MEN WERE IN THE DAY FEATURING ONE
EPIPHANY REGARDING DAMAGE ASSESSMENT

XI: COUNTRY MUSIC .... **C**

XII: FINIS .... **CVI**

I:
TRACTOR BLISTER SONG MOUTH
HAWK VULTURE SONG DIESEL BEAUTY
MICE SONG DESTRUCTION SONG MY
TRY AT WAYS IN

///

tractor of my sore throat

///

sing

///

tractor of my
weird ass light head
because pissin diesel exhaust
since half the hotshot world war 2
pilots' blown vegetable caulked hearts rang
the bell in the bloody bucket can only swim
and foam some sideways silence and foam
with a crimped little fizz loop the loop boys
fly to sweden fall in love for the days

///

eye of my eye sing
scale of my scale

///

there she sits a
broadcast manifest sits the center
but with no real list to 'er

///

reader beaver bailey care to
itch yr bloomin
hive rash on the wall
til she falls

///

eye of my eye
scale of my scale sing

///

one war stone tree diet giant's crap
solid as that

///

400 gas start 1956 diesel farm-all tractor
humped up too near nowhere to be shut right

///

where's yr outbuilding for things like that

///

where's virgil to u rah rah all the reed rash out

///

where's theocritus to knead the knots from yr flesh
the little pine pine spiders from yr flesh the sabertooth starlet's dimples
the tornado pressin down on old calico lake the
little slipknots musked by paddles into the longest face of the river

///

whatever it is you do when doing
go and tassel a little time to the top
a little breakdown time

///

grape that pea if ya know what i mean

///

friable affirms the firm
castigatory artery
aerial vim
zip that

///

unseasonal sudden and still
it's a professor of weathers
she's one stalwart wart
all in apocalypse gesture
she's a dinosaur she's a dynamo
carbuncular turncoat
graced with cyst names

///

trust it this
i ask you sing it cuz
maybe i know the beauty
foghorn better than
black ink this is my breath
everything really
inside the dark song
cardboard bugspray fires
them secret seeds
one shaky answer
arrogant yarrow
of tomorrow you are it
the future fulsome head

///
trust it the world
to miss the point
that digs to sign
they will say he must have something
something to sell i do it is a rotten balloon
above where children are and playing the tree
///
of balloons of breath their given puissance
///
to reckon circumference you must first trust against mechanical means
///
uncommon movements and no gloves
generous blisters then
offer unseeing eyes of legitimate water
///
and who will slake tell whom to sew the mouth shut
///
not like the country much like the man
///
the puritan bodice spent sing
///
mama mouse
one blade at a time
a tar hide tire to cling to
one blade then one stalk up up
a chaff at the tank
was blown in
a wire chewed
a winter's nest
the teeth of time
can't be much different
how it all bends
talkin stalkin
the common prayer
save yrself
///
what's that?
brevity stretch please cant

///

shittin starter's shorted so bypass it

///

sing river of flesh in a man's back remembers
the turbid bled and floe the jostle
of the mechanical bull it is the land
once turned once tipped gets recast as sea
it's one big bay coy oat cove sculpture
its furrows about to crest to crest
just some old out of breath ox acre
at rest in the rheumy eyes of octopi

///

the shittin pigeon the shittin gull no the obviator albatross

///

have you seen a father carry a newborn into the sea?
first time for every sacrifice dreamed
but you have seen a farmer walk a newly tipped field
staggers yr swaggers
in times it takes to break the free toy

///

sing the hawk the fish the crow the fish the bobolink the fish

///

can afford to
fly like yr dead
when what yr after is dead
buzzard
but hawk spends
to fly deeds the wind a life
perhaps an aero boat
pace just this side of oblivion
perhaps a beauty in the year 19 & 60
starboard elbow propped
trails a toe

///

and you ride a deeper dear and smoky whale
a never quitter there her rare old beak
time laughs at no laughs at time smokestack laughs
crude boil fallen in forest jellied by time
and blown to smithereens
up the chuffing stack

///

some guys post exhaust pipe rust out
when they've suffered enough facesmoke
when the dry cave at the back of the back
gets licked gets kicked by facesmoke
some guys they'll just put a length of pipe
so long as it clears the limbs and sheds
they'll just put a pipe guys will and
let 'er smoke ring a crow
wobbles final there beyond
the so called reach of man

///

and what's a manmouth
but an animated and sputtering fossil
but a diesel glitch all those days

///

and you are the one
when the masthead breaks
for chance at twice the brandy
agreed to be tied there
and what you have seen
none have seen
dark spots
dark spots
fires for brain
fires for urgency
for hungry for urgency and
blacked by depth's iron nests
in what sometimes seemed
a ceaseless acrobatics
of storm clouds plunged under
and circling and hurled and bent and beat and chasing

///

those rocking and whirling hours
those yawing gape east years

II:
STRING THEORY BABBLE PERSONAL
CHICKEN MAIM WEASEL BODY MIND
BUTTONS THEIR FATE VOLITION THE SEA
THE SEA MAPLE NONFICTION MULL
COYOTE NO MONEY FOR DUMP FEES
TEETH MORN LAND FARMS YOU RAT

///

now then there's the man south of town the man and
the cat the goose the dog and the pet turkey
some puffer fish in a magnifier dream
how he'd convinced 'em all to swallow a string
with a ball of meat a ball of sticky grain
how when the string they shat
how he'd onto the next
until cat goose pet turkey and the big dog named rob
were all on parade joined to a string and how he'd tied a tripleknot
out the ass of big bad rob
and sometimes'd take 'em in the bar or just for a walk up the road
to the cacophonic honkings of the amazed

///

and that man got canned because he was spending so much
time at home cleaning shit off a string
that man holy misty kept a bar
of soap by the garden hose
and cussed himself gently gently
as tho to pull a sliver of sheep wool
out of a baby's eyelid
cussed for his bad back bad luck and
cussed for his own stooping
but gently now there's
a decent rat pride there

///

to name the direction of so many

///

true a string ain't a rod but does it say
you will and this way for now it does

///

until what exists exits acids that string into not string
and it's everyone for their own alone again
the babble kin again the sore mouth kings of
the rushes and weeds as i have heard
as they are known to tell through a shoehorn mouth
through a soda burp gotta pay
for the water but it's all the soap you want for free

///

our body is
such a small thing
fits neatly in a trash can
but the mind it emanates

///

i myself have been at the bottom of the sea
with one claw from one crag opening
unlike the bulldog face
of an iris against your shirt thrown over a chair
whose buttons speak
to the nightlight's pinched but steady heart
of what buttons speak of
of disconsolate disregard
that you are forever touching them
without feeling them

///

so reach down for lift earth
so pat it into the ledges
of the dice so fate rolls
so hum a sweet sweet thing
so crate the dog articulate

///

but then attention or the rum
a companion with an observation
a companion with a gripe
a companion with an urge
a burning at the nose
a stomach at the throat
does what it does
offers an elsewhere
or the self

///

the pecker high and melting snow woods
of the self

///

get there can
some sap gathering buckets
galoshing yr feet
but how return now then
the sap buckets sapped up now
the each bucket heavy as a body
the glad silence of bucket
via their purpose satiated not unlike
the dog-end-peace of a drowned good man

///

and the strangeness of the tree waters in buckets
and the lake waters in he loved life

///

how not heavy sink how not spill how
when the weight you have become
in carry act
drives you like a blade
any blade will do
the bread one sure
into the facile ground

///

yr story went it it went west it
died on the trail
it ate a poison berry or twelve
the snow and slush
in patches only
gleaming quality of light
incites some queasy

///

no no the story's rite it's
thigh deep in the head alright
plus this real snow melt freeze to twice wad web you

///

but wouldn't ya rather strap a
couple dreamcatchers on
skim on above sail on
parse the forest in a lush no worry
skim on sail on
like the proudly religious call
parenthetical or beside
the grave nakedness
the death obsession
the place names translating to bellicose
censers afume on split spilt bowel stink

///

that you may sit with sap
companion it over fire over night
the sapper's hot seat
the insomnia of syrup life
think of that
of a life
beyond season
of a sweet dark life

///

old weasel hardly knows herself
hefted up brimwise
on blood all new
she dried the chicken
of life's liquidity
she's gloves filled
to sopping with old aloe ocean
and time time's a trial
until her lighter nature returns
until her whiskers
sentient danger thatch
squire the choirs of air again

///

chicken run how
is a is a is a
now you gotta choke 'er
but not too much
else she'll flood
cough a blue boo hoo
before she steadies out
in roar

///

in a near bled out man is an armless man
the legs ropes on fire
the legs like funnels of ash
the legs as bad connections of ash

///

to fritz and to fizz

///

pray ya give out in the tub pray ya ain't
a royal mess wino pillowcase clucker borne
on the moonsun of tragicomedy

///

and what's a mouth but a meet memory machine and
what's yr mouth's handsome ratio? as per destroy vs reify

///

pretty as i am i am compulsed to mumble mar

///

more bite down please it's for ever every dip you sway atop then
corkscrew a la the owl your neck to see what surely was
that you have cleared the gate

///

tractor loud enough right set sing
little scraps and threads and patches
of nonsense priest doled hypoallergenic clown noses
from china by way of tacoma
press 'em flat against hands and
did they honk a little? a little
in wonder over early ice
as the geese do sometimes
in early may is not for me to say

///

'ractor slow enough to
belabor anatomy again
the lines in hands alien
landings and launchings
the robin redbreast
scratch and two steps
trusts her face to the dance and dart
to the giving it there

///

every little pinch pinch and pain
choppy land rolling and flowing through
yr body's flesh
unbraiding
braiding
bearing it

///

the land sounds you
given a motioning over uneven and broached and breached
land farms you
touches you
tractor and dips
a tongue eye in every word
of land and of you
yr between legs radish
carroting
ploughs you
disks you
prostate
xmas light
drags you
rolls you
flickering

///

are the hard in the crop
of the clucker
wrestle in the sack
with a bug
all the nights
of your days

///

are the corn and soy
they say hear it groaning
should you use the dead man's shoehorn
for strum the dead man's chest hair
should mushrooms nose
a dead man's assertiveness sugar
the bones of a teen blown longer
than some trombone glue glue gun cheese

///

a porcelain candescence god
some shop lighting blurting urges
must hurry from here

///

mizzled grist
what the haybined grass
how the down grass would say
midswoon if not for the roar
of the smokin whale
and the bang and whir of the bine

///

if god is
god is a
coyote trailing the green plume
of cut and thrown headed out timothy
slaloms to catch at shredded mouse
bits flung back red half
alive or not popcorn
beautiful dream
the ocean movie-candy store
the ocean amazon.com
the wave windrow live green lava
it'll eat yr center will not hold

///

the beautiful logic of a stitch
nobody's dog does
zag 'er way to full tank
and timberlines in the
tautology of hospitality
we meet to beat the prolix superflux
slap the icecream ball in yr mitt
throw

///

one idle bee
chainsaw wing fog song
holds the cream up
one flung sugar drum to another
boys if that ain't the sun
then heat up the skillet
and ditch my feedhats in

///

water and flame
they say can hear
same song in each
hey the ear ain't responsible
for the candle yr brain
the crayons melted and melted and
sloshed in a coffee can

///

saddest person desires
to eat the self wisest
knows the world eats and
solipsism is self consumption but
let me ask you wise ass about
what is a body to do with itself?

///

two teeth down the hatch in a bar fight

///

your decent teeth descend yourself without
any hand help from you there is a
gravity and a life is suction auction
nimble toe boy down the silo ladder
ling ling

///

wait out the mystery
wait on the tight so
danger turns of the self

///

unsir dentist slash taxidermist in the perfect present
puts pillows on the paws of a chicken lovin fox
not to worry says he he'll handle the enamel detail
says he's entirely capable of settlin 'em in again
when they come through back to himself
says when they do to throw the teeth
in a coffee can with bleach says
set 'em somewhere you will
not mind the smell
for could a skunk hate himself

///

late at night in a truck whose barfy mars song
stretches beyond the county late
at night late they squeeze
out and pant because
the heart is carp and they
ease blown tires late
they east trashbags
into the ditches

///

one yellow phlegm on an aubade would bee
to stethoscope that tire
no that one
for nothing
hum eats hum

///

but the trash bag does give a sound
with a name try
fire of a bargain basement flag
dipped in the creek til the
colors piss down over
the bones of the sheep
just as white as your own
if blood be a mirror
glint the skint is
a shimmer worth its weight
in creep

///

this is when you rock the
creep feeder the lambs smashed over and this
greasy squirting rat gets gone by going
like a frightened thought shot dark ah leash
lease fleet fleece grease ease

///

and where are you going little lit rat man
going with the chasers chasing
as tho that's a cob not a kernel in yr mouth

///

ah open the sides of yr hufflin rat mouth
a little now a little more a lot let the breath in sides
kernel tacked tight
tween your uppers and lowers
fogged soft backside where yr breath gets to pumping
in the lang of the hustle and hungry

///

a kernel a cob
one for the many
mostly it's lefts here to dixie mostly it's left
me expel a miscreant seed leftover
privately upon the tissue
down the clarion swirl
this lemon tea seedy wonderful glad to be shut of it
open to anything

///

and life life is a paper airplane
its milknose blunted
its children wildly
out of flight flash more dive
occasion of a room
its milkwhite walls
bent to bend the sucker out of flight
the beauty of children ten strong
and growing
like monsters good ones
next never rest nor sever
paste race grace
glue will do now go
and go again again

III:
ARMY SEEING FIRING ROCKPICK
ROCKPILE COUNTRY SILENCE BEARS
BACKS TRICKY CLICKY STUCK PROPHESY
MAIM SADNESS METAL MONEY WAR
BIRD LUST SUDDEN ONE RAG GASCAN
RED TIP RED DEEP AND SO MUCH MORE
YOU CAN KISS GOODBYE

///

down or up
death and death
vulture vulture ain't you just
one bare bone more than loosely
related to dirt

///

while lookin level lets a limbo
lets a soldier trained as welder
solder you up with secondhand breath
and grateful for it

///

and what is the armed army but a lot of running early
then a pill prescription
then a shitty back end
in terms of the civilian reentry
in terms of pay and everything else

///

billboard says help a hero get a house

///

all you got to do is serve for that tag now

///

no in the old days it was do something heroic for the hero laurel
try save a guy or three
get a wound keep alive on swamp water up through yr nose for a month and
come back all the way with one elbow two baby turtle
shells over yr kneecaps with 4 mile to the helicopter and you was inchin
for all the world like a dog man like a broke dog

///

now it could be all you did was eat a camel's eyeball on a dare
there it was
eyelash in your shit tomorrow
like a civilized tapeworm today
yeah now you can come back covered up in the lice of hero light
i mean itchin and scratchin
mind you not havin done shit jumpy
by the wretch a wreck to see

///

in the kid's eyes the kid's eyes are hearts
and what's a sketchy heart but a bird
but a bird with a radish for a butt

///

nothing more holy than seeing many things severally
yr thoughtcrock can't process have to live with yr eyes a little
and yr eyes are jelly flowers and
yr jelly flowers the roots drill nilly backwards
so what you could know waits to know waiting still beautiful tickle
this flood food is cents for beg a dollar
after it dries on the rocks that is
can't thank fire enough can't think
number beyond number

///

so acknowledge this on leashes in the air above you
everyone you have ever loved floats and kisses you
connect and thresh and combine until everyone you have ever
lives in a floating morass above
hissy heels kisses you airy
what would you do
what would you have done

///

passed her on the street and turned to talk or to see her
clandestine as tho in a revolving door love revolving
the eye's appetites satisfied in a whorl not unlike
the habitation of the snail they got it
doodled on the exoskeleton snake suppering
on snake

///

age the pencil
take 'er downhill sure bird's wing lines
to the terminus germane take

///

and what is a heart but a bird butt sewn shut

///

hand's lines
are scars
we're born with
the prebake we come from is a toy farm
plastic butterknife plough
improvise is it
kind tone mints
better brain a butter dawn bird
with yr grandpa's long bone so to gaze
through to querulous glazed

dusk birds so very
radiant and wary
from whose hard mouths a spidery
web upon whose single-hairy snow-
flake one more tightly more tightly held
moth

///

moth
enfeebled tho it be two two two
two as any one with wings beats beats

///

blindfolded man swallows
at the pace of each each beating
his race heart this pry moth

///

also the orgasming man how is he not
in his prick's vulgate releasings a heron's head
a dying moth outspread and going
on and on about water

///

do you not feel that you are drinking as a heron wd as you yrself gush the human aloe?

///

now
the firing squad assembles
now
their unmasked faces masked
now
the one with a high voice complaining
of having stepped in dog shit steps out from back behind the outhouse
but that's what you get when if
you dally nigh the tower of shit
is kicking the ground
now
the hammer backs
all the hammers back this is
some easy work the last supper they all
say never can you
taste
now

///

nothing

///

but the sawyers have it much worse i hear what
the water and the bloody sun can
lift from earth so much harder
than one worn out played out man not in the forest

///

and falling

///

the one you could shave yrself on the shadow of

///

the other what does he mount to?

///

hear 'im fall? slab wood in a mush-ouse is all is all

///

india she has her rag pickers
my cownty we rockpick
so many old stones new this year again
frost uplifts playing at
rocks picked or exploded
the tnt the ropes and on three
it is the freeze and thaw
spits anchor loaves new and through
it's spring's baffle mouth
its monster glass jaw dainty as
a dumptruck size of dallas
full of bull cum the bullheads swimming in it

///

dusty dust this soon to be disked field
unbent and visiting
with my trick back knee

///

so watch what clay lei you loop yr timed heart thru

///

midfield edgefield woodsy colic rockpile
lonesomest because deadest save the feted because harmless
grass snake lain dragon loin my my

///

guess a farmer back is an old dinosaur mouth
come alive again and
what's that yr chewing on? guess it's a little

lava seaweed compote guess i sense we grunt
at the bottom of the trialing sea
sense we are under things or
hectic things bulge and wilt
big then quit between us
and a sky mottled with breath

///

what yr gonna say hear it
before you say it all the old words some the new
upside down and caught up in one another
or phlegmatic or starling or lightbulb or bat with a weeping disease
wasp nest thought tack heart paper
or hands in prayer trees in trees the birds may
will the world circular but higher
in every tree another tree busted and gusted in
like crazy

///

as a wrinkle is
a crease of days the motor moan
a truck on a road a card on fire
get well or the jack of diamonds it don't matter
put it out with yr spit you can't escape it out here
sorta tugs at yr odd shirt like a button of wolf cum

///

as a feather dipped in any empty bottle of dip spit
kid'll never forget it the room was dark the morning early
the flat soda flat? something dark and low
in a bottle evening cradled swig worthy worth a swig
now when the father floods the son prank
when the heart like a snowball studded with gravel
grins does not grin guns

///

my apple's white now every otter page another smear
i am somehow this presentable
for how it's been as i shall tell
with my stony snowball heart with this hawk
feather dipped in the salivated night uprearing

///

to the tune of the wandering black bears of this earth
the wandering black bears and all so sweet
shit the open books
everywhere they have been
and turned a mouth to exposed

///

as prophecy is a condition
of the intestine
if you don't go on yr gut then how do you   listen
how he is now to how he is

///

billy p by name one with his heads once upon his field

///

under
hawk
and
sun
he
lay

///

lost arrow bow haired over in time harrier hawk
anything inviting bodies sun

///

this book of my napkins up
upon yr winter tree key hand book of my
dirted and descending mouth falling
for years for yours
for and in the language of rat tunnels
runnels down under the peg head barn not a single solitary
nail in her no

///

with the chickens beyond
these human ears with the chicken
breakdownchat whaaat laughbladder

///

that corn chopper sucked his reachers in and held
held until mangle won as chickens run how
and lift the skirt as land that's damp wet
like in a mouth like in an eye unfolds
between you and the house
encyclopedic kite
in the war room of a dreamed wind
rattling its foil teeth against the cold
death breath through it some twisters rising
as springtime's snakes do

///

try the bird thing twice
unseam a misty crag home
through which ultimate licorice wind
pulls a thread of aspirated saliva
is watered fire tire deflating soon boom
wrecker driver up all night
toeing the ditch for freckles
was he born again to spit?
his eyes as tho ironed with ice

///

and the fun yes just waiting on just you
with the rain on the grass in the yard holding
to itself trembling everything
shall fall for itself for its own weight's needing to
or else the indiscriminate criminal wind

///

because your cuffs swell
to the frozen chicken
weight of handcuffs ungainly with tears
because you can't swallow those
because your nose is a hill
because there are caves
because the leaves
blown by the wind into the caves
tell without ideas
of a new desert
of being in it
without a wind
to push a first word out
as a mother does a once only child
pushes her whose thumb has yet to pour forth a milk
towards the other children whose bowl
of squeezed raspberries are getting squeezed
are blood only sweet see

///

and it's all between in twain
you and such house pleasure such finer joy
it's the rain voiced
to the temperature of the wind of the fatuous wind
and the rain need i remind you
beading many on the blades

women men sweating
some glass eyes not waiting
to get at you
where yr blindest
and blind you
some more again

///

that's a bird toss of laughs exploding
features antics of an animal
every other aside does
fiddle drawl fabled tomcat try
all one steel string
turned tight tuned tie

///

forgot to shave something somewhere loosening
plumped or pulped
wet or dry
anemic iris
like a flower

///

and lift so no low hem sog

///

as the party is some
about removie all land
from yr physical parts seen

///

dry ought sog long

///

and sun tawny little rabbit nipple of sun like sun
no other fire none more timely

///

bite kickstand
junk it out for metal money lay
like a hammer or socket set
oh a busted ah a sat on
repeater function candy cane

///

far from the dog on the yard with a bone
sounds like he has a future in plastics
a plastic picker pissing
his white and yellow teeth flashing
his gnaw jaw like a hand claws
down through old gold mountain
is my favorite prayer isn't anything
can't be gotten into
and rocked and picked

///

deep dream hard on teacher gun
swamp a haunch swampa   hoo was that
tried farm the edges of known
to swallow dog or man more or less at apple handsome
back in there and willowbroomin deeper
back on the rollin sexfat bogback

///

old time fortunate cidering baldy
grows toads
only tree i have ever heard
to pick itself
like or as
phlegm up the nostalgic

///

leek breath nimbus occlusion
enter field but not locked to working
short clipped grass tell whoosh
of the workings done the lover partridge
beat that winged chest
feather handled door
in thick high woods
off in

///

it's a amp stamp
for the hot heart
for the mouse thump
for the wild strawberry for the radish radish
for more than mere vegetable fear

///

between fieldholes
from home to home such a trial such a candy cold sandy mush and what

the muscle and how the flurry hurry how wool how save
one wordlong mouse with the hawk mind you
like a birthday cake cake beaten at with coats saved
or so the story rolls
from the house fire hawk
all frilly andiron and
pumping down

///

impotent innocent potentate with impeccable aim

///

how a nothing any body is
not dressed in wings
how a nothing flying is
how long and obstinately still the earth
how black fear floods the meat
likewise the squid the sea
this vascular instant this pluperfect cry

///

brother you were just another 4legger beat out by distance

///

hawk when you
explode upon the earthen fleer
with the milked ash of a glassed milk shattering and fuming

///

then i know again
what fury is a
condition of
foot and mouth

///

each feather fathered mothered
but where now? hoo now?
guess they went vent
out through sky
like a kleenex to flame
like a priest on a leash
in a tarpit full of criers crying molars
full of holes where the sugar insistent
as a carpenter bee at a rafter is it snowing
the hard stuff the feathers
each one brilliant lazy and
unfair as justice is a lark over a battlefield

///

a wound an active one and flowering
from the gascan sky larkishly
tongue out pulled out
red rag no hardness
go on and say baa baa til the cows
trombone construction cone

///

bounce and the reddest redder
bounce and grab for yr jaw
memory of a painful word
gets to drilling in there carpenter bee
is it snowing the hardest thing the softest thing
charlatan can only cry little lines
of sand drawn in by pupae dying
of thirst with a chicken feather
up her ass the dog could scent
the merit in the croup

///

pansy recover may she was carried off
is for the birds indelicate asymmetry tough to stomach
the trash you meet in a circle little junctions
of handshakes and hearts
cupped and duked
old cash was born
to stretch beyond

///

it overwidths the palm
it dishonests any fist
we care to balm

IV:
MORE MONEY MEDITATION SOME
HYPOTHETICALS FECUNDITY CALL
ME IF YOU HAVE GREEN EATS WHAT
LASTS MOUTHS OR TOES THE HISTORY
OF KLEENEX AGAIN THE RURAIL NOSE
OUTOFDOORS THE FUTURE THE PAST
DINING SUFFERING POKING AT GREEN
EATS WITH A PISSIN REED

///

money changes seasonally i wish
wish it turned red and died beautifully
think the philanthropics of trees
wish every rich person had to feel that debt shame stone
firing the anxious sky field that on yr neck
that neck back burnt in perpetual prickle slough
feels like it has a life of its own
like it breathes as a very old man or panther breathes
his teeth gone his beard dirt sprinkled on breathes
a spider web over a guillotine
once the people made a deal
with poison's keeper

///

yet the fancy wind
through the torched
touched web
it chanteth on
chides no charms
skinny cartoon fingers
of fire asleep alive arisen
we must have them not too close now

///

just as light to the touch
as any herald of no insurrection wind

///

cash wish fish full on gold
sounds like a sinking
onto the tufts of the sediment and wrack
where rocks would have given themselves
to the gorgeous dressing down of a passing water
by glitter and wink say 700 years
rock from toad to cup
the sweet and slow indenture of the U
if not for the farm run off
the leeched shit the sediment
the good fin blast occluded

///

the miser at home
so stingy he wouldn't give his dog a damn name
feeding dog the apples
and the oatmeal's silverfish for a week and change
applies the hot gilt as we speak

to the dog poop
soon to cinch as it cools
for the holiday party
as a joke oral paperweight

///

and i wish the poor won the keys in the game show of life
won the keys the car the thirty foot long car
the rich applauding like babies
chance shined you tacky little winner
of the thirty footer

///

and i wish the poor loved to make love in the 30 car
when the leather is reclined
and the rain gets at that adamantine frame
size of some vacation beachside bungalows
the hood open the cap
off the windshield washer vestibule
the rain having mounted it and mountained it overflows
the beardy brains of these peonies

///

these flowers these poor
find here and there
thistle run on bromide stuffed
down in the sweet little capless vestibule asshole
and the morning hole having been dug and the poop pooped
and the hole covered over and the mist lace
these natural curtains of the day ghost flirting
these every person for themselves beginning
to realize out of the mist as 2 not 1
their shared hands make 1
and the V of their handheld arms
is a neat little redneck martini of light is
loving to float a little hot shot
down the cleaned lines of the V
down the earthdark olive of a chanting's bright

///

the sky its leggy
reach beneath

///

takes tools
and a dying finished
to learn
the poison throat

a clay swallow
the colder earth
abreast and full
against the hoping green
yes the hoping green o the hoping
green

///

the heart roughed mouth
eats every language for fire
its lasts at first splaying
pig-faced flame
succumbs a log does caves
like a windbeat iris from whose
hangdog droop drools a sighing bee
whose body a bearded fuse whose
mission a sweetness blunders on

///

there's yr standard oblivion
in the guise of the sour breath sleeper rising
towards waters made and the waters
hung up in the pipes waiting go
as they came like time like smoke like love

///

nose yours one blown outside

///

to blow your own wet
so it seals and sinks in earth
they say put yrself out there

///

if what's up in there is past
if a nose an archived gourd
if a nose a spending gun
it takes a rain to shut a bird
it sometimes seems
i take aim at ghosts with ghosts

///

moi being one such hickness sir
can blow no mess
on shirt pant nor shoe
the mucus free to gloat of
relations with a spiritus
orphan goat spackle

///

that's a clean shot
there's a music to it

///

the world
less dead mouths than dead toes
can't get a ratter ack math than that
when i die plant a toe or two and see
what grows perhaps uno neurotic aspen
whose whole soul goal is to shake it
full flusters the wind

///

the world a mouth
grown over as gape is really
all there is

///

so where was not a living yes for yr waste juices

///

but the parlor linen crowd saying
tote yr snot
hank yr pank
and all that crusty jazz

///

for ex
the hank to kleenex move
one such unjust degradation station saying
a known nose a nice clean
flesh lint trap
and ya better treat 'er
as such bub
of the handsome
struck-a-spark
lug luck advancing

///

to play possum apply a temp shroud and blow

///

a science of the unself unthanked
some godly times in quotes

///

while the kleenex generations charge
on credit a clinical and cleanly

banner unfurling you yes
you of such little faith
grown huge on the fogged
glass eye of god free to
throw yrself away haw
haw haw
haw good
luck with that

///

to be seen and know it
candy but a bad bing
go choose burn to it

///

while the haw above a silent A
dug slug out damp ass stump
while the haw hawk
stabbed in yonder
cancerchanceblack pines

///

to be poking at yr supper
with the ultimate minute
and second hand

///

a vengeanceless fire line pissed
pisses a vengeanceless fire line
hawking

///

one hawk screams
did god just bust a branch
of fire of creation over
shit's junketing knee?
one hawk screams

///

and chicken and dog and man
turn jerk jack an ear
depending upon
language fear
wind and damage

///

but the bud brother of sound another sound
or silence with a loud wide thumb with a sweet dumb smother
for the fun of smothering

///

upright man's brain drains fast forgets it
bless my mossed flint toes for what?

///

for there's a little mercy in knowing we hunt each other only

///

while outside some perhaps many or one just one with
a populated chest sings wild
and green
i love you i kill you yr toast

///

wonder if
every tree ever absent
world a golf course a dream green
where men can aim and get volubly
murderous about errant orb logic
would world this still host howl if nothing
wild nothing to get behind
would then sleep we sleep never wake
sleep right through death by thirst and
the one thing probably we'd be dreaming

///

wild river on whose coffee counter 1 3 7 bosom bean rides a toy tea set

///

oh he lay bet on it threaten ing
to cram his go figure actually in land
at the thought of her long before this day because
of her condition then fresh as a popcan
of grass in a sheep's mouth
before the innards black a say

///

he membering the buckhorn
tavern where lost his two front teeth
lost every day since man what a racket
ragged toothfairy moth hovering

///

it's a helluva snake tail gargle-athon
to wonder all yr life where yr
teeth

///

from flag to rag in a heart skeet

///

and were they in him still? and what the attraction? so why not
show milkwhite faces? the teeth perhaps
knew some stuff some debt weariness were
sharp or sheepish shy lout lazy or did the teeth mistake
some lost highway of gut for a gestation

///

and did they pray and in praying not pray because pray for themselves
and their own alone in the main that
he'd shat 'em one day
the size of tombstones then
the moon'd inhale 'em yes
so deep in the skully gut of the moon they'd pee
oh yes deep in the shapesome sharpness of a precious catacomb and floating

///

to whiten the whitest black the blackest
would live and die all at once dial interjection
at the most broken silence ever unwrite
a name like they were handin out paper in short
go deep god beaver for the flow flows
til it don't timbers all
to a one thistle beard tit bone burn

///

and he he lay fingering
up his upper gum
with his second or third strongest muscle
with his tongue with a memory of

///

released from duty's circuit a human body buzzes oval
a vacant building its flies a sandpaper lip its flies the wingspeak of
the mouth the wing the song a nothing
or production in destruction
angina angina

///

some new have rag air to chaw a lore rum let

///

the air a little black then clear the rice explodes the bird poof dust
the old moon old enough to baby that lippy river

///
lake over the road
its quaking crystal hem
much thick with tadpole twitch and pulse
///
lashed to the past i crap this present for u

V:
CROWS FOR PETS ANCESTOR SEXUAL
RELATE SHUN MORE HAWK OBSCURE
VAPE SHUN MORE BUZZARD BOD BLUES
COLLUSION WOODTICKS GEESE ICE GAS
SIPHONING TRACTOR CUT METAL WITH
SOMETHING NOT MEANT TO CUT METAL
WITH WHEN EVERYTHING IS BROKEN
NOSTALGIA THE MANGER THE MANGE
AMATEUR METALLURGY MOSQUITO

///

for he had been one of two men some the north of town
known to men to have tamed a crow i tell you that crow
followed him to church sat on a post and out they'd come and there that crow
would be waiting on a fence or on the hood of the car
that crow a coal a sheep baa got caught in and his

///

half and then maybe 3/4 the congregation twistin their necks
in the jailbreak talkin hustlin for the car before one
loudmouth or another crank caught 'em in did you hear how are did and
twisting the necks of their hearts the people swelled a little with envy at that crow his crow

///

it was the closest thing
to having a really nice car
two little oil drips for eyes and a beak so big
dream head gavel laugh her huge
with a lizard's stray strange moo moving

///

in frickin short a naked snake killed with a bible slap crow
was nicer than anyone was a hundred pound of noah rainbow in that crow
was a good thing out past judgment crow had his back
what's that barge of timber pontooning in yr eye? it was right
right nice to feel that little fleck little crotch of good night always
out past judgment bobble bubbling in vision's edges always

///

to sit on a shed rafter while he cussed a machine to get at those
belts you got to have yr wind yr cuss best and the patience of
some sturdy char in witness but that fool crow started in on dandy
would star glide away midfix to go on and run its bright head puddle wise
then dripping drift back in above and carrying on
about how lazy the rain work drop wait til
ground give a mouth party until ray lee laze until
the whole shittin tin shed had a echo about have you ever lit a lawnmower on fire
tried pull the cord fire honestly maybe not even
close to the pest pecker echoings of that crow and his truly

///

lay a socket down lay a sweet little necessary wrench
the last straw upon the last crow

///

turn his back to reach for what have you and his
crow in a shutter of startling fastness sudden rush of blackness

as the night is rainin jellyfish as the jellyfish are plastic trash bags
as the bags are plastic but with the falling power of iron lead
mouthy cocky gut wild lee falling
like that like death down came
fool foe crow

///

all floating out across the barnyard and lord knows to where
the crow flies with something shines but i'll tell you if
there's a bitter image for the witness the searcher the faithful it just might be that
crow 11/16th wrench out its front side shine freckle first star twi lie
and swallowed down the woods soft sonant ketch pie

///

talkin everything broken foal duck dirty
for a stuck little big broke ass tie

///

and it was then he knew a life without options
simple frank rock bottom balding the bottom line

///

so dressed himself head to toe in a blackness borrowed
a few things from his wife but that's another story and
slid like riding ice into his car such that he fooled his crow
hoo wasn't easy foolin its bright eyes dark upon him
fooled the crow that it was a funeral
when everyone busts their inner crow out ha ha
but the sorriest part to report is as his .22 rifle reported through ka ka the
dutiful guts and gutsy brain of that crow his well what can i
tell would be right

///

he had a heavy brand of sorry heavy all his life

///

on a shovel flipped he his crow into the woods where lord knows
his dropped for losing airmailed wrenches creeped a stellar blow
like a mule ear peaked locked bolt right light against work

///

everything out there against that crow ya know
wary for the taint of 8 fingers it wd be that way forever four three
and then a three four and then a four three and then a three four
yes was a long one before the last black feather fell out
of a straight line to go on and seek the sleepmeats of a circular dust and rolling heavy back and
ford in deep wind did that crowless crow o you could see the lefts of a wing lift little in storms
you could see that with your dinged ear even as tho some sweet black loam to swim tried

///

just a fin not so fine and a-rolling did the sue see dark

///

a lesson in glisten passin wash by wind soar
heaven staircase
of grandpa faces
accompliced by step meat
hell escalator
coxcombed in
turkeybeard urine
man that botchy brood had a way of getting down low

///

but could a sexual
window remember it lent
opaque terraplanes to the unrepentant sea?
the sudden restraint hint
of a jowl to the stiff when the jelly
leaves the jar dreams legs for cordon pardon
part and sail that tripping hawk

///

a moled sun then
a slipper dagger up a hair
went up natural
came back brass
ah then then you will rise
pinkie the crusts from yr eyes and say
as tho coo and clue were one say

///

ain't farming if it ain't breakdown time

///

where yr the butler
the maid and the mess
true nose
farce wharf some say
all that is is the bone under
and an ephemera of skin
an assuaging of handsomer clay

///

ox pox opportunist of the gust
born to live both eyes open

axle is to sex a wheel
ax'll wool a tree
in the book of the leaf
soon to explode into handsome flight dust
along the creamery streets' storied resolve

///

your power
and yr punk corral dissolution a prophesy for us
the machine bangs
your hearing
what? the lifting
of hundred pound everything
ruinates your beer beef cheese
gutter better screws bone spurs spurs in the glue bath
such that then or sooner your back needs some slow walking down

///

saw jammed on backwards so it'll roughride the metal
needed parting apart the sparks
inside each a metal mustard seed beak
getting at the eyes

///

get the fuel siphoned in a hurry
that one needs go yesterday
it shit the bed yesterday that one
just layin there where the high grass kicks in
with a laughin belly full of fuel
with an out of work blubber butt
right now it don't have thoughts
just objects rhino-ing across the rind

///

get some fuel hurry the hell
yr supposed to suck in but then
let gravity get thirsty
let gravity piss easy
takes care of the rest tolls the troll
with the tetanus gong but listen
this tipping point oinked on you and in
went the fuel so acci-gulp so shit-spit
so spit-stick-fuck-a-pyre so the paper towel
along the jaw along the inside skin

///

still it's no use everything
you eat for a week
gets fuel dressed sunday's
casserole walks in in a newsboy fuel hat yes
in a raw daw rainbow
that's a true for always and any about the animals
you can taste need go while dine need go
so it don't piss where it's standing for a home

///

bone dance do the
bones dance
off the slew foolfoot of a clumpy buzzard rising
with a deer leg off the fatuous ditch buzzard whose
business is the stinking bone loose
buzzard neck sewer pipe and one
limp scatter trailing after
so a dangle looser dangle plays
some deery underwater legs role

///

sweeter instinct least in a zero we may stand
when men slowdance with their tools then sun more than
a drowned nickel try skinny ninny dime

///

with a redtail hawk with a redtail hum it
patienting the wind
tannin hawk treacle-ing the wind
whose heart must be a tiny brass bell
flipped over for cobweb out tea costs nothing
but a little company friend coasts prone delighted syruplike bones his
magic silk cheap at auction a thing
picked at by birds and the other after dark rovers with
the bullets of snow poemed and pyramided up in the slim jaw

///

and sun in truly in him excellence
in his shut eye parts some red wafers pooling
last two poor fawn spots rag moon lost where
in the high grass wafers dual combed
fox on a fire ramble
as random as fire
catching at whatever's dry next

///

taking tastes

///

what is the yellowdogtooth corn
what is the ballroom gown
clapped up in a word in a book
clapped and leveled by luscious dust

///

in the dank trample spoil pen
listen like kissing after drinking to those are
the forced feedings all across america this morning

///

with the wainscoting of the field
peopled with crapped out rigs
just some boil wheel ass half implements improving
towards a satisfaction the bog bug bites on
one defamed mange face wanderer

///

in the hour of the waif and wastrel
will mizzle a wilting
against stauncher tooth and tine
pour some light on there
get the seniors out get the picture made

///

by the tractor
thick as a choiceless life
we seek name
to make or keep it good brand
the fenced in this year's chancy green
by the tractor weathered down from
original candy red
to first the rusts of flesh
the rusts of earth

///

way back they dug with skulls
yes the sawing jaws of
how thick this skull
had to be
to house such brush fire howling
and not crack

///

yet it's in fitting parts too
you can watch the skull's
suture lines itsy swab along
drunk thru spring snow
a ice out on the river
the sound of the ice going
when it does its first undo clench
all the guns and then a shuddering
buckle bulge hectic ecstasy

///

first goose and coming home
a baby goose in a shot goose
by the opening river threw
a back out in shouldering her home a shot
goose in a kitchen sink baby goose
in shot goose in stainless
all the rage back then
didn't fit made it fit

///

a ice out on the river
do the neck just so
a drunk itsy thru snow
a glass a gallon kiss
do the neck just so

///

enter wooden roots
to drill and stir a hope
if i pass this way again
the learning to unhand
the things that lived
what's harder and
out of our heads
both less and more ourselves

///

a metal for consumption-ing
and booom land open
the plough tugged open it
dead bomb got mind
got thin

///

the fork and the knife

yr no longer a little one when
tips and edges
sharps and serrateds
can't seem
weapons we make nice with

///

eating one stabs one's face just not quite
and over the stone fence of the teeth
an offering
along above against upon
eternal the yoke the tongue
built everyone
the fox and you
for teat O thread of
a white three falls
crooked line
from above ranging
the uncharted woods
of skin to end in blouse
wastey lichen a little musk lake

///

up from beat
couple hundred million mosquito
nascar bag war
nosy needs flesh's under river
buncha palm kilt nothings
bugger after tractor time
hang on wind
in the open arm posturings
of the skin seed wood tick

///

is a living button
thirst its cause
a living button
its 4eyes
the thread
corset penitent
there is the body
a leather bag and there is the mouth
attached with no pain
drinks in deeply
less and less itself
so is the button
a progress

or is the hole
buttonholed
one's heart's pour
in its mouth
the tell-all
made by hands
missed the boat
ethos low
only touts
a swinger's couch
a singer's thread
the stabbing action
the purple mouth

///

i used to think of what if a mosquito if a skeet bites me
and the dog and the rat and the bear of the beauty in
such rare couplings a little knack shack
fanned full of warm strangers
next year's next life's sting band

///

now i dream winter's washed
dried and put away white plate silence
when bites stop then
a head its own season then
its own pair of dice bossed then losing it? take and whiff
old musk lake the wrench no cunnings
it's just what you will lake
spring turning summer
gathers up in the folds of a packing afternoon
the sun a mouth
more than hand the ring on with it
allow swallows
your finger and you'll never hold
a thing the same and what
you are capable of holding
is another way of
unspeaking your name

VI:
BUCKHORN TEETHTASTING ON THE
PASSAGE OF THYME CHEESE ORPHAN
SPACKLE TURTLES TIGHT TURNS DIESEL
WILL NEVER SEE THE DOOR CAN TASTE
IT EVEN NOW AND IT'S BEEN 11 HOURS
TRACTORS SEEDS DEBTS SEXINESS THE
INVENTION OF THE WHEEL IS TIED UP
UMBILICALLY

///

and the people laughing
all the time at the animal crafty
in the story the animal theirs
but always throwin
their name off
a hat in a sudden gust
the mercury flashing off
the slickest sucker back
in spring come up out of the black black river
the silver red blinding sort of
in the fixed mouths of the people
the gums just awful
the teeth punky young from just
couldn't leave off and so turned to it
and so turned into it how many you know?
bottles fleshed then flensed
up and walkin around
their faces flushed like inside flesh
just came out for a spell and caught to stay
buncha bottles softer up and walking around

///

the harvest all in
just having stepped over to rice lake for the reason of some extras
to salt down the machines for the winter in a shining
lube so it was a strange thing
as he was a take it or leave it man
as he was about the only one in the whole damn
silver jaw swale gum county
could take or leave just one
when he peeked at his son his eldest
who'd helped him to haul it all in to say
let's stop for a couple at the buckhorn
that was after it was the bloody bucket before
the moccasin bar that's well
it's been a long long time

///

for it being not even sundown or close
open up the door the bartender he would always remember
was the size of a bear but not a spring scrawny one an honest to god
full up on fish on berry pull up an ant hill and guzzle it size
of a 'cano bear
one of those men if he so much looked at you

swisscheesed yr shadow all yr wispy starlight pouring out
in a marriage of rice and bugs on the broken slat board floor
and with some shit ass beetle shovin white all night along the underside

///

and these two other guys in there at the bar at that time
roaring kind of cackling at and eating
at their lips at that time the beer the brandy so hard in 'em
it had come out of 'em through their skin
and into their shirts so their collars lay there
limp like a piece of lettuce at a pizza hut salad bar at midnight
so it's dead pleading let me let me back to the water phase

///

knocked the one guy barely on the rib with the elbow whiff he did
and he proffered very reasonably without looking over at all
the sorry having been said by him at that time
for minor elbow whiff
to the arm or rib of those strangers at the buckhorn
at that time says the fat ass lettuce collar fool
hmmph and he sits up like a chicken off a new egg
well says he hmmph and he looks all around
at the nobody he's boasting he's cutting the heads off
the hearts out the livers out of the dusts he's nibblin
at the intelligent livers of every dust mote in the county at that time
shot through with indian summer snugging sun

///

usually see hmmph
i don't usually accept no apology no apology but
seeing as you are getting to be an old man an old man i will or put it this whey i will
have to pledges the drunk trailing off to taste at his collar again

///

jumps off jumps off
and he jumps off his barstool
maybe as tho he had a ghost seatbelt still buckled on him
for he was never known to take no guff
with his son's eyes simultaneous swelling tremendous widening as tho a dead man's pulled wider
by a terrific and racing flood

///

for he kept secret hot rooster salt in the olddog pouch of his ice heart listen
punk hotly

///

looks like a yellow streak a half a mile wide down yr back

///

and i may be old enough to be your dad and there's no
doubt in my mind that you'll lick me but when we
get through you'll wear my brand

///

slaughtered pig that drunk hears him out eyes him with eyes
everything taking a long time because
the very air is clay
like radio tower lights owl-itus leather coins poppin his eyes
man above hear them skin seams squeak
why don't we factoryfarm bears? fact you will suffer
for the sweetness of yr thoughtmeat gamey
keeps you for your own fine wandering

///

ups off his stool like a refrigerator getting turned over by a man
in a machine deep in a hole at an appliances landfill

///

rough like fetlocks cut in two like to use that for dental floss
they go

///

beats his lettuce lip head
upon the floor like a gavel gave rudder to
the only schooner in this swell sea world does our hero but then the
unk shuss sucker see he has a brassknuck on his sock
one pop and his two front go
go down with the wash

///

bear bartend in a flash remember it to this day benevolent tree
the mind drops this acorn on repeat the drunks by the scruffs
and out the door and i don't know
how the cat shuts her mouth with all them tongues in there
as the door flashes with white light shot thru with
as a drunk two drunks and numberless dancin dust while
him on his knees runs the blood like a roof in melt season
and the bear bartend dancing
like a man with boots of ice on a fire

///

and the great wide bearlike man he proffers a bar tool a rag
he sacrifices one for the benefit of man

///

careful in his thanks as a muskrat is to the trap he fools

he rams that rag up in there and
he was sure to pay the man
an extra 25 cents for the blood stopper cloth
and there it all begins
and so it all begins

///

the wondering where they went
and would they ever return those
prodigal front two
it's no way a doctor ever would say
take yourself and call me in the morning
with his son on the ride back nibblin at his own lips
as tho to try and taste his own piss and vinegar rising

///

yes when people partake in killing the thunder
of the belly people they kill the lights
in the eyes shut to bite
poor food
very poor long ago must have been happened upon
it must have been an accident
a wreck a mess a food or
the tongue own wayward and wandering un eye
a tooth a milk densed a brace of flowers

///

say cheese say if the moon had skin
and a carpet foam of fat underneath
ponderous orphan phlegm
it's a hard on the body it's a little new religion halter
a for airy a chafe a
f for false staff stab at uneven ground f
caulked the castle all night but i still feel a little drifty
tickle quince johnny blows chunks crumple and blend
where the bend should be the nose rag there
working its way out of the black pocket of the man there

///

what is that nose rag doing tell me
that older faded red rose nose rage doing   what is it up to as it does the double of a leaf on the
yard in the wind with a crab crawl liquidity arches back
held by its crusts in the oldmandrunkface folds of a flower is it
down on the yard is it embarrassed over the house dog's deuces is it just yard day
it is in exquisite collapse
rake like a mustache on a teen lain lightly
against the constantly giving tree

a giant in a fairy tale besotted on winedrunk farsighted citizens
their bedlinens some stuck between his teeth symbol sails
upon the gingivitis of the sea of the sea

///

something to how strawskins of green to how
several feel holds one above at is dirt
cat dead bird murdered badminton birdie
barrelhousing hard that snot in yr blood
that's sledding on a newspaper sud sud suds
blur new old honey holy finally against the ass of fun
ho those ducks fat farts blow the pant brown

///

do it the good old blind way   say cheese bye
and a group suffering mood vibes back
thick milk clay moth nose anonymous

///

is it dark in its whiteness? is it personal? it is
what we've always been doing and will do

///

a call a mist a cleaning a separation
cheese space
mother between a rupurration   mother and child
kept apart
a hornbook a clot a clook of skin wanting to
brutalize the nipple for grow
how they stand the pee
our own eyes bubblegums clenched between the molars
of the ammonia emanating ol shit hill
has some sleeping to do on fields far as the eye
but piss like a bullet in the ground
can't kill the dead twice
is all killdeer brokewing at the noses

///

say cheese tag suffolk thick we supped upon uh uh
waterlogged walls rats swimmin flood winnin
little and long bap bap white rat lines
as tho the life of flashlight light
living in a slit
lays the belly of a lightning contents seen bald and flat and open and found to be
docile as possum lips
the lips not the incandescent icicle teeth mind
asleep in a snake sleeping the high and tight sleep of oblivion
bell vine gulch where the little thing goes? went

///

tractor dear may you frickin forever churn full
like a turtle lives forever free fall old
water's a catchy relaxing atmosphere
and the turtle in it suspended floating
an idea not an action
the skydive free
the opposite of that
were to paint it would paint it with
water no one would see paper wilted
is no good for fire the oldest hotel
the oldest hotel elevator each bing a
going up old person picking high fruit
very old person very high fruit

///

so goes blood through turtle
their one blood
share it at night they pour it
one to the next at night turtles
their mouths tilt then touch
like children with dolls
simulating lovely love

///

tractor refractor ever whale
i musk i wrench i will
coo roll ocean door
rolodex window
in each flop and slap
a mother's son's son
and the sands inhale
and the sands dream of pearls
in the ears of etiquette

///

farmer sailor whaler adult butter knife dragging
behind whose son's son's
speed too much for the turn
of phrase hides
helluva blind
turn pain pill pain road
hay hawk turning sky
a ray can opener
and the scalloped potatoes of
a vigorous sexiness spill

///

a definite fish
split from the school
the waking in the night
taste of diesel at the spit

///

in the language of a fantastic castle
at the drawbridge of the skull
not a swerving
into the life of the machine
more the residual of a diesel combustion
more the shadowed shepherd of the vowel A tastes
more burled than birdly
string of xmas lights
die out random
random and rainbow
caught in a sudden rain
one umbrella between the two
randow

///

tooth aches too soon
early poor
smoke stack mouthtomouth
old muttonheart pulpy
ask the bog barf rheumatic
for redirections ooh to the blued sea
ahh to the sky's bruised knees

///

implement kicking dust
the now and again bang BANG
a big rock old dead glacier startled
into crank and what if old stone new seed and what if
planted
what will it bring of
course ice god this blind cold grace course
to sore an eye with squint in watching for a sign

///

want one? one what? dime
this is my minimum face wage
the slap unheard steady
as the river through a fish
city construction silt
far from here pastes the pace

in a race to ungrace

///

that's debt's iron hand glowing red
a dawn or dusk
demonic hamburger helper
the power to swat power to pinch
as a child pinches
first one wing then another
then another until they too
could be seen for seed

///

said as seed
laid down fie low shallow
storm of hair above
us finger sun lean
tip sun
some good frickin grand canyon sized apple
blossoms beyond the dead mid of life
when a person starts living again

///

as youth is making
a gun of some fingers some of yours even
and stick it in at the bellybutton
and the workin years then
you catch sight of only
when yr truck windows get so
they need clean
the dirt holding the image in
yr shoulders bunched and tipped
as tho this one time is punchin you in the gut
o cold as a chemical thought up
and made to do just one thing

///

some swell hot fat pinch beyond middle age
some hardshell fruit on a caracol cruise control
soft exposed soft variety seeding in again
in the second revelation of water
in the water that sticks and the hawk hay brown
that hair lampshade
salty sap sweetly suet
lost not gone
roosts in cross mouse
vacuum for haw portrait

of a correct decision to go to bed early
for posterior austerity
lay above him upon a puff of wind
sexual part
the shadow of
ran the zipper zig zag open

///

baby maker par
plastic window thrown on a fire
the clearest grease that is   the war rocket
thumbed to a crying the exploding death
knife has feelings too lord
lord

///

and it shall be down there the feeling of
as tho a hand scooped deep in the creek
comes up with mud stone and water and that's
minnow shy darter's pulsing gills
the the the the the the the the fleshy echo o' a heart
the the the the the the the the heart itself necking
the the the the mouth needs go round
for O
the circle world
of animal and thing

///

how else nurse

///

the wheel invented by bellybutton gawk
and you can write that the frick down
the mother the memory the broken heart the song's i
thank being down wrong for wet my throat
and stretch almost giant the tune is
in a skeleton eat talk about my kingdown
for a cage yr transparency and the mouth
the gouged eye socket off a giant just mentioned
offhand optical lock grass
eyes two new tomato volunteers off
to the races all square makes us human
hearts from this angle circus life

VII:

A MEMORY NEVER YOU HAD IT MAKES
LOVE OF THE BODY OF THE SKIDSTEER
OF THE CARCASS OF THE SOFTNESS
THE HARDNESS OF HER LEG OF A TRAIN
OF BUILDING THINGS OF DANCERS OF
VARIOUS KINDS WITH SOME NOTES ON
FORGETFULNESS MORE PECKS AT LOVE
AND CUTTING UP A DEER IS A CRAZE
DOGS DANCE AROUND THE DANGLE THE
DANG HOLE VARIOUS AND HUNGRY

///

with his wife before he knew her
stepping off a steaming train
with his prone mouth twisted a la one runover plum
while he's guiding her now the v of her falling foot falling now
the point the tip
into the only other place besides the heart place
it's warm and folded and falling in
is not the murdering of desire is not anything but
a perfect smart perfect because accurate and he he
a little thing filled with an air fill hole
unplugging his being snaking
under carelessness of youth
not looking back not one hangnail glance bursts
where she done dug in
trained white circus pigeons
freaked white silk kerchiefs burst from him
doing the every which which way
everybody watching shooting is shooting
is playing his mustache for a gust string
the wildest dog in the sovereignest woods
the water spigot in its mouth it's turning on

///

the gypsy family they do a dance on the flowers there
have them stay off their heels have them stick their arms out straight
like a hulking cross has them
have them in shoes that come down to points
put a paper carrot on their noses have them in a rising mist
from the heat of the piss probably
something so recent given
to the world by the living horse
something so recently of a body
have the bodies of this beautiful family
force the ice out elegant frenzy against freeze anyhow

///

and sew the steady eyes seeing the sewn level
breaths of the thoughtful bearded builder
it is cold to the wheels of your cheeks
his beard seeming steady him
how the belly of a shovel pats the ground down
he who distains his crew of muttonhand rowdies agonize
over making this and this come true
the cooked fleshes of a breakfast lingering

in his mouth excised by Tsquare prayer
and the swallowing he's doing
without knowing it every man a waterfall every tasting
of the teeth every bird a stone skipped
from heaven a poem scooped in if it is true
death is a general silence then why aren't we all the time talking
over the top of each other

///

passed her on the street a living poem and turned to talk or see her
clandestine as tho in a revolving door a lovely revolving
the eye's appetites satisfied in a whorl
fishin for my supper
in a whale of a time hole

///

the throw of wild animals
over her shoulders
and the wool stockings she wore
on her legs
with her left leg falling towards the 3legged wooden stool with
the one porter in 300 miles managing to negotiate into the one place for miles
not covered in ice snow fetched and toted 8 horses' piss there

///

with a heavy parsimony with a diesel chortle to the motor
like a rooster with a lung cancer on the d on into
the shin of his field   a leaky PTO hose but that's just natural
for the age of the machine
d d d swiss cheese hat tossed against semi formidable wind
maybe 18 and a half steps in and rolling and
was he a puddle of delight in animated reverie? he was
and did anyone ever slap the earth make the puddle jump until it was as syrup is in its own
sweetness shut

///

they did and he was
like a dog in something dead
and fate face raked by wind
by trash bird by the late at night rovers with
the bullets of glow snow pyramided up in that slim jaw again

///

carcass is done to only
makes no choices
hitched to the hoist
the bucket on the skidsteer elevated
the winter quiet the carcass a picture

from the shadowless window
it is painted on

///

so were you born to dangle like you were painted on
graces empty or fill emptying or filling
as the coat skivvies down to ruby and marble
of flesh the men wear their coats like the coats are wearing them out
the wood smoke and the pitch o' the creosote
the black heart fire amen
lord but we are exploded upon amen
build more than they take down
their knives thoughtful their knives
almost sniff   their knives never forget a bday
an anniversary maybe maybe once one
day erases one day ice the solid ground god's tall thumb
god yr petulant and frankly fatuous eraser
then looking up tho some of us some down
gaff half frumpy into the middle air   achieved by the skidsteer

///

what that leg could do in his mind in a time before
anything about their life the kids like a living fence
against rosying about the pasts the kids a wedge
to keep a person out of the pachyderming of a moment
from the past from
the humps and bumps and mumps a drive
a field a sudden tiredness a suddener
lust to live a little across time a little
maybe big hawk skating across littler
birds dip and pick passing bigger bird
the past a bucket with wings maybe
when teeter tips the sun lites up like a plate
passed through then down a family
what victual what slop
fermented and tipsying then did fall from it against him
the woman wave

///

maybe the stool was gone maybe the porter was
just machine not a second fleshy aspect but of the train
he sure steamed like one like it was maybe a mirage
after all of horse piss and gypsy heel tap flower smear
green no don't shatter now   now
he was the stool her stockinged foot the cheap pretty shoes
hurt her the shoe and stockinged foot the white wool leg falling

the middle moments when the leg was not hard
seized to brace against the blow of the earth in
this case the stool this cased world and he yes himself slid
in in place of the stool when she was in purity of motion
the flesh inside the wool unwound from the bone
of a tightness that newness makes
of a youth tightness never seen again
her mind all words and light farm duty
bent on the week to come the lessons of
and he wanted only one thing that his groin
be at the spot where her foot hit

///

guess all of life is
some guessing but he had a better
sense than most because the mind in the world is cardboard furniture
if you or anyone breathes right everything changes and everyone is always breathing
but the mind in the mind is some more concrete and a slow mix bag and it happens
just right he's only breathing in it's only natural

///

with her left leg falling having left the shuddering steel of the train with a drunk singing
all ragged along the street below when the street was an ocean
for the drunk unleashed a hiss of sea piss
but never missed a beat of a three song shore
his song mouth friends and strangers
ocean's refreshed lip of crimson linens after war twist untwist
the fabrics held in the besalted furious or lazy raise and fall
in that tipsy ledged ocean animated damage cloth
jumps binds unbinds every hoarse promise
for a peace inhaled up the salt hasp is almost seen to speak
prayer or promise my remembered make can't ate it

///

her serious sleepless sister either praying or touching herself or both
as it has been said board never leaves a builder
totally behind just as paper is fire friendly fire from the sun
just as a leaf is a creek whited out with underwear pat at that gangrenous myrrh
coining
never gonna collapse never not gush sun bunny sunny funny honey

///

in a beaver ass and the leggings taken from belly of a deer
but first this stool towards the school week with the leg falling strong
from the elements defend it the wool stocking in
the years before he met her knew of her
worked in a roundabout way

with her drove her in his father's model A
got stuck thrice in the snow john green leaf
drove her to three dances used his hand with her hand on hers naturally
said to everyone and to himself and to the cows
and to the trees the steering wheel too that was
either cold or hot but slowly the temperature
of his working hands
said ain't she the lim-it he said

///

skidsteer born in manbrain
to hoist what is
beyond men
in heft used to
in their first open air design
tip over
many men dying on the ground
under the machines kaput a man
mean or kind a gleam bone
is not the hardest thing
the names of the men
the names of the machines
run 'em all together
in a mashy gleam

///

a semi pullin kitten and bee upended puddin hart war shore shout at

///

what you can forget you can live with
the cutting mens' chins in the air
in the air and guiding the gaze up
the air of the lofty
the knives from here fingers light
from here like nothing else
beyond nature almost unless a cloud
a sows' belly of rain a silvered hog clag
unless a cloud snot running out of mens' sleeves

///

one timid oink bestrewn and bespattering
like a wild ditch flower of many sung
in the living hinge of folded tissue box there bumpin
heart rides wrist like a limb beset by drop fits
of rains three anguish storms collector of
turbulence's quenchable jewels rides
the rest homes of the tree

///

no house no
drain no drain no strain
o this soft whine of the dogs oh correct it over to rest stops of the trees
o is a dog just all our fallen private hair wrapped around the first
time we built a fist of fire might might be
gathered like goats around the skidsteer
and the men in a gloriole engine of flies
the men finding their way into the deer
fire sculpture the warm snow of sinew the one big heart
the men unhearing some sight backcasting
little sinews little ribbons little inbetweens
little glue spots little sightless eyes of purest white never
hit the ground untasted they go down the gullets gone
of the dancing dogs with their
woundy flower mouths like this this this new again
hatchlings almost all mouth everything under them
almost beside the point opens to an opening to the sky
and to trusting in whatever comes it's not gravity
it's not a pity it's not even quite hunger
it's the freaked trust that's life it's the automatic
urgent hole atremble for fill and filled some sturdier
amounts to sing

///

the goat dogs dancing this
whine like rainbright hinges on a gate a gale when she's gone out back
past the manicure when she's gone to meet her lover when
she's wounding vegetables along the indent and then there he is all clenched
in his need great big eyes
great big need which is bigger
eyes or need ask the bird if ever it gets enough to side it will
gate or gale it
will

VIII:
CHEMICAL HELL MONEY AXES THE HISTORY OF PEOPLE PENNY PINCHERS THE HISTORY OF BAD BACKS AND A STEPBYSTEP DESCRIPTION OF HOW TO CURE THEM FEET OR OX STRONG MEN

///

with the sprayers inching
with the sprayers huge
with sprayers the shape of a death bug
sprayers all night the death juice to gash the ground
with the dead junk sprays
with the sprays singular of purpose
the destruction of man is simple
the plough is not a fin it can't bend dead bird nest dead bird
dead mouse dead vole dead frog dead toad dead bird
dead flowers 13 kinds
with the sprayers hulking
the guy in the sprayer waves
the guy in the sprayer's daughter
with a guy at the park
by the water pining for the daughter pinned
by the moon skulling the water
the moon and the water have no choice
the daughter has a choice does she
the plough has no choice bloke bludgeon
the chemical in the sprayer no choice either
actual monsters are invisible

///

when everyone wants to know less than they do
as variety is a cuss
what use what's the use
efficacy only in unknowing myriad
dumber us tv antenna never quits
slurpin spray efficacy
burns a cradle
in the toaster or
could we wake?

///

but nothing i tell you is hard nor more not hot enough
to unwrecklessgarbagedress the destructions of man
unless a stone and that and that
in exploded chips lives in the thigh eyes of the trees
messes with a grandkid grown
his chainsaw chain snapped and his chain bar all twisted by a secret stone chip
in bed with the water turned something like stone and
what's a tree but a cast agua in an ague baby goose man above that
pretzel for a soul nut hail tree
must have been underground one leviathan
the size of hell or a house or a ten horse barn

one there's no digging around
already wore enough woods out to go around

///

happier with a second use
now that's something in a circle is lost to all
your cot in the basement at heart is ruthless pollen stag pinafore   dizzy bee
hazing over clover hoods of green and white
it's life just life at a squint and action

///

for the wind a name i don't know
hums i am the train not a soul
knows what i am hauling it could be shells
it could be the perfect rounds of sands to frack
it is not the sand in the sea it is the sea in the sand
in every sand piece a sea rides
in its belly a gulp of mystery
even to thrive is such a surface glide
now i never met an unwise butcher
a tongue to a roof glued
invites the train inveterate
to spoon noodle for even
in clockwork
lives one or

///

and he lay a snake of ant curve commode runny envy
in the bell of a bear fart or five
from the middle of his life and then another nine tie on
lay exposed maybe 7 manstrides from the ditches
on his prickle hayfield just about right there
where the kids drive through to party
are countrylazy and kidlazy would never think of
not driving the 30pack to the little carton and capgun fire where the field dips
and the cops'd have to get out piss on fire for
a finer smolder wash yr hands with gas after greased
from some monkey toil on a bastard machine is tradition
a fiercer fingernail i have not seen on sun's mad beard
ho the cuticle the engine? how are you one of those haunted by a touch? finger's
series of boring bones a road? the meat of the larger
hand the middle of fuckin nowhere? the people out there
smoking and staring at their phones like people everywhere? did you just
put yr fuckin smoke out on my fuckin phone? did you just down-
load the effing ash app?

///

the old time people to gapmouth enough fruitfleshlight in to wedge an ox in
ox and wooden plough in no one needs a thing
old ox needs hay think the thinking persons of the future of the past
would not know dirt if it bit 'em
o bud it will one day dirty be
tenses for ear
a thickish deafness
there's town strength and farm strength
know it like a bullet thru yr meat

///

it's to the ax we sing
and the smoldering stumps of yore
life ain't fair shim it
the circus comes but once a year
and everybody who works for it eats nits and ear wax and such
of a whisker chaw hole for a body
of a pillow in the hard times and riding and rising
of a bristle born from a second cutting bout 4 and
40 days before this sudden indian summer sun
butterscotch embryonic ooze
the hog nose hair the stalky field
a bed of nails it's the proximity
of pinch and poke in close calms it all down

///

and they were shut of the river when they could be
a dry people but they had a wetness
in the mouth and about the eye
and that was enough for awhile
if you dig a hole the water down in there will wink
and that was enough for awhile
anything you do the water does back
and that was enough for awhile

///

no shame in stoop for the heather of heaven
mr lincoln's sunrise burnt beard

///

lumbered like he knew how to money worry
but of course doris done all that
what he done was the worry
the numbers in his head had been
darker water sudden fish face

when a mouth was a very gory block of ice just trying to find in
they was ain't they was berrypicking when this sudden decking belief snow
went to swallow gag throwback fish fate face
from a time when nothing swam swarmed flew or walked with grace
from back in the sledgehammer brutal
mouth like a headlocked body roll

///

windchimes of good bones
hallowed by the tongues of good dogs now
the clatter clabbering the numbers good in his head now
and she had done all that never had a violent argument in their life
all set all square and he just made sense
from truck to where he was the ankle of the field
the gift the theft the field
the safety from a double-yellow-eye woods croucher
the trigger of a double-yellow-eye winger on high

///

his steps those of a man knows both the heat
the heat and the cold of the land
of the people less than the animaled land
silver dollar souvenir pilgrims
savings accounts careful leviathan sporting blimps
lumbered like he knew what a penny felt like

///

no shame in stoop for the heather of heaven
mr lincoln's sunrise burnt beard

///

in this sense i am my father's mother' father's daughter's son
in this sense you are the daughter of the windiest stone
best word is the word won't quite come
together the tray of trains fingers the snake between
the legs of the con moves when the town line'll him jolt clean thru

///

why do things the dog wants fall for that
if i am the thing i am thinking wind rich with
petrified especially lithe huntresses
of a bristle stackin electric up his overskinned spine and down
of a trim shot stalk dream of a porcupine bloom if i am the thing
and the dog having rolled in the lively dead soft softly approaching
and the dog a cotton crime about to happen
a moistured mouth i think i know i hear
one tongue like time it is it is

it is work to chill? i am the thing i am
not thinking the dead can walk time

///

while the work packs the spine
meanwhile the work packs the spine it is surely packing it
a hasty cram job slow and sure
a packed mash
like a fresh pack of smokes
is that to be cool in 1957 or does it perform a function?
people will tell you it burns better if cuffed
this is for how you feel shorter than you are
hot froze mud tramped by bored wild animals
is your lowback it's not just everyday motion does this
are ducks in pain about the sky? is water the only healer
is fire water a fuck quack if i ever did cry a spine one
two options to pop 'er back to true bust back did you slide
on that inthepark homer exactly wrong how's yr pinch
how's yr crook does the creek in you have a bossy name?

///

someone stronger than you
come behind and lift you
imagine a carcass dangling
try for that
relax like the dead eventually are after
an acupuncture of mushrooms shakes you
the living ox man shakes you
shakes you until your spine explodes
hyper kid at a sheet of packing bubble sheets
gives it that royal drop and clutch just right just enough ah
breathe again without hinder split
yr ribs suddenly not some old plaster of paris
exoskeleton folks made to kill the pain a little of TB
didn't kill it

///

or and this is more domestic grovel the gavel is yr tongue
the judgment hisss silencio
lie down serpent huffing dust
down and she'll or else
one of the kids will walk your spine
the softs of
either side
their arms outstretched

sorta like a fire walker
oooh in a sleepy troll boil
you pontifical portentous you
nothing pops frantic
just melds in all is
settled with a step

IX:

AGRARIAN CONTROL ISSUE DEERFLY
HORSEFLY HIVES GOTTEN THEREBY THE
TALE OF THE ASSPINCH GOOSE THE
TALE OF PISSED TATER MUTSCH

///

if something wild with eyes teeth a mouth
is a chance that's what a farmer hates
if a gun is residual of a people on people war
then the farmer pumping lead into the corner
of the pasture shoots beautiful
bruises blooming lichen style into where his
once wing sleeps time after time out walking
thru the head high grass why a buzzard
has a face i'll never know should be belly
for brain
ditch the little liturgy about life is six inches from downhill
get you a good stiff slick sled and
clamber back up
pancake exertion worth
the world eye child can't wait lean
hard miss some the stalwart tree again

///

up with the wind fingering the 30ought6 hole hole hole hole holehole deer xing the the the the
in his 27th year of the hives
at ration caps dijon white glove car door servant tray
up with the grey poop on honey bee is not an option
is an option
skin trouble
flesh sick
is his face an un washed pan
and sun the egg his face
ol horsefly deerfly all the biting all the bitter
born from what was born in
known more for what it can hide
bred at and blew from
toad usin toad for a walkin cane

///

honey buddy close your eyes close and spin
here's barf in your nose is so necessary
when he was just learning what his skin was
and was not
sick little swamp seeds with a bloodface obsession
horsefly deerfly
fly close pepper atmosphere nose at ear inn
and set upon him and step up upon him
biblically locustly yeomanly

///

don't look back is so true
how they do pursuit
prize fighter in 19 & 19
dukes up spoof
describe a sick little circle cyclone
sick little bowing circle cyclone
inside of a wasp nest
the guts of the universe
the worm the hole the corkscrew the gusto
isn't any different
than hybird of tick hang in
greed need and spider
rider ride the
slipstream signature
bankrupture cur
cursive cruisin
little cove
sank stag at in

///

and set upon him
47 to the day in the near
near by way of crow
the road on its back
only road that is
is a crow's back
we are slow dough asleep
bit bread awake
somewhere in between
the crow to walk the plank
of our baking body rib eye bender
that the old fiddleplayers and organgrinders knew
crab varnish how crimp a finger-set to
that there's an obsession ocean in the turnip of your heart
ancient venation scene tay

///

catch cliff cracked clam crow's-feet
ain't we all a little prehistory
glean gleam bangin on
hoo hoo's blood you usin this time now
bones vs soft stuff
seem a little mommabone to me in the tonight
of those birds throwin a lotta carryin on

in the stones of the oaks above
the body broken gotten
out of the road

///

he'd planted once in corn
cleared and rockpicked by
an idiot with an accent
made him seem relentless
when really only this little rag of land
the skirts of it heavy with the rocks he'd dragged off
humped 'em o'er there the tree shelf mushrooms
in his low back all a-turnin to cheeeese
tradition
when you quit with anything greasy
wash yr hands in gas

///

the man down the road a slovak so he talked liked that
handy gas lean

///

go to pick up the man's milk and
every time clock work his yard goose to sneak up and
pinch that ho-bunk ass
as he leaned his pisser against the rear bumper of the milk truck
help with the hoist and slide of the milk cans in every time that goose biding
like an electric string to get as much bunk-lo asscheek as it could
in a corndog cattail chopped in half worth of goose mouth
and then from the mouth of the one who could talk human
always as written on a stone with a honest to god stone
y you dirty son of a beaaach grabbed that goose by its tried neck
and twirls 'er like a lasso pillow let the dream scream out hulla
throws that goose would hiss and shake would walk to compose
his goose self as a cough sometimes is seen to be settling a wearying frame
until tomorrow the goose eyes
the britches the goose eyes the britches the long and silent lively lived in neck
the ass cheeks hanging low like eyeless siamese angels with no way to know
what individuation or vision could be so they were beautiful vulnerable so they swang
low so the goose like a clothespin stranglin a bellows fulla prankster frankfurters one bite and the
room explodes with particolored sawdust now that was one hung up and spicy tree shade haunter

///

shoveling gravel for a dollar a day and they'd get a good load
for old man mutsch from down the road to spread the gravel
so everyone was not all the time going back and forth on a swill heel hole road

so there was some pebble to it so it was tacky so it was not cruel old
man mutsch grew the best could say kindest potatoes
such that people would come from miles all the old people gone now
would be there at that season at that time lifting beautiful white brown potatoes
as tho loaves or little sweetly sleeping baby bodies from the soil
leavened in horse or ox dung those spuds spoke down
to bombs did not know what hit 'em   no the dirt did not dirty
no they rose clean into the working hands the organs of the earth
the perfect earth the clergy surgery and old man mutsch sitting high
on the cart like a winterfatted bird upon a haybeaten nest of futurebird
says come along charles was the name of his workhorse
but that horse would just stand still as a horse of wood a plank clap trojan says school
no farther down the word along than the letter L when old charles p mutsch esq
lets loose a stream of pee surprise you anything could hold
such a stream as that as tho a body a pond AND a river

///

o us shoveling boys would laugh and much at mutsch's expense
the old man's face turning a shade of red that was new to the
eyes of boys like it was painted on surprised his face didn't bleed out
and such was the order of days until one time
old man mutsch says i'll be back directly with spark to teach you
boys a lesson spark being mutsch's dog barked all the night
furious pockets of bark all over the night
for in each pocket a worm
for in each worm infinity hegiras surely of
wolves or bears or coyotes or wolves or bears in the night that or
the dog was guilty of the imagination a nose a coal a fire flamed head
now how spark held an eye open in the day after all that none could say and then
back comes mutsch after the 20 minute or so layby the lunch made
by the mothers of these boys the butter sandwiches heavier than a hand
filled with river stones as the hand is coming up out of the river and
the stones you could say are held to be pissing river

///

and back comes mutsch and all of us puttin ears in our eyes
with the red in his face dripping back down his neck as tho to go to sleep
in his balls probably which are two chestnut cherries from the days of
george washington on fire for or from a concubine boys load 'er up
says mutsch and we do go to shovel like hell as tho wooling some ghost
on the lamb and we do go get 'er loaded high in a jiffy with hardly a huff
cuz we are boys and hearts are elastic apples you could say the wind
of the lungs will waggle the apple but nothing breaks the attachment principle
with a tidy crisp peak to the
gravel like some kind of coning hat as tho everyone everywhere is
thinking of slippy pyramids solidified dawn to dusk ancient egyptians

bound to blind in a gold gold creased grin then sez mutsch
go to spark and claps his hands together complicated like he'd bruise
or milk a prayer

///

man spark that proud dog leaps squirts freaks squeezes down sunder side under
one great fast low motion doubles through the wheels a blue heeler see
delivering as if in the silence between the flash of bomb and flesh of boom
a terrible nibble against the horse's ankle if you will willie willie
that old worked out played out sag nag of a carved nothing knotty pine gunk leaps
pretty much out of fetters someone threw a hundred
thousand monster motors in there in the innermost runts of the river that horse
man above gnashing that road in a flood go and with a vengeance entirely new to the boys
like watching some giant sneeze marbles not one peg nor jot did mutsch carry there
where he had meant to o all fell by by the time he got there to the there he had in mind and
mutsch why he lost every article of clothing he had to the wind of the motion why his
eyebrows clean rubbed off by horse speed and mutsch he shined boys like a baby by a half mile
down

///

road had the gravel every marble of it uneven like and for keeps
so the road for it could have been a month was a little more jumpy there what
they called mutsch's testy hill and
not where he'd meant to for it was according to the happy rage of old man mustch
and to spark who had the piss turned to wine in him a foamin mouth of it a winkin brim

///

o us boys in the backdrop herniating ourselves
with laughter bent double and some triple as tho to clip
own toenails with own laughing mouths back down there
where the creek did what it did back then and lushly

///

was really no lesson to 'er or
maybe a man could provoke a beast with another beast by one word or two?
or maybe a pride is some fierce little little teeth
or is it our rage makes us new
bears us to a newness on a sudden third foot that won't last?

///

or is it well to know our feet
to face taste them
when beside ourselves
with glee and wonder or furor
our feet out there every day
and what is a shoe anyway but a cottonball

in the ear while the song of death
murmurs up out of the turf over
the slowest accordion ever
stalks a hawk with a honk so low
if we are lucky unawares
swinging low to the living chain worm
yes the ever famished satisfied winnow muffler
shall us exhaust yes
in our second sleep so clean if lucky

X:
LOST TEETH MORE SOME POSSIBILITES
IDENTITY PLACE IN TIME AND WHAT
A PASTORAL PILE OF SHIT COUNTRY
MEN WERE IN THE DAY FEATURING
ONE EPIPHANY REGARDING DAMAGE
ASSESSMENT

///

where those teeth of his
and only his and gone so long?
or had he missed 'em? truly kept an eye out peeled for
thirty thirty heavy heavy breathless change years
a stick a sumac heron leg stiff poker by
the toilet in a folgers fire hydrant red to the purpose and should he flip
and should he graze?

///

but was it possible to hurry the disasters the distances built inside the self
via the goad of pasture grass or
maybe the body thought aspirin until nothing happened
or maybe the self clinged to self?

///

his 2 front rabbit chompers by now rougher than a cob probably roiling
in the water table somewhere probably the heaving action
of the earth the roll and tumble
probably one day they'd plant themselves set root
and drift up a flag a pylon to silence a paean a pie don
drolly calling in the executions of the mistake cakes by the red bib
beneath the white bib by just one slight sly flip of it or maybe
they was visitin roadside stands inside himself still
maybe made the stand owner
a leetle tadpole kettle nervous way they leaned their starched white lightbulb elbows
on the papery talkin fly wing in a brittle poke par wood fruitstand   ponderin
the tomatoes a little too long and was there a record of every breath and word in
each tooth and were they too weighed down with false promise and flee and fleetin puff to do
anything on their own cept loiter with a lightbulb goiter angel

///

and the stand owner twirled a clutch of his own beard into a knot
resembled last year no two years ago barnswallow nest
breathed and the teeth breathed and the woods breathed
and it was one of those long dramatic movie moments when one waits for the murder and
cormac mccarthy was somewhere out there behind the 9 hundred thousand dollar camera eating
healthy because
he could afford to

///

or indomitable two they were love love lovers
graverobber had a rooster tattoo on his back
head like the sun had a rooster tattoo on up his back
along the spine a series of seeming windblown musical notes towards the sunny brain
grave Rob had a strongback girlfriend named sandy or jacki or sue
and if she did not dot the eye with a heart then you can kiss my leather fish

///

she kicked for the football team
said she felt a peace in forcing flight
with what she walked around on
said it was a waking of the foot
to a higher purpose   said she could
conceivably kick yr asshole into yr mouth
said lucky for her lazy most people already had it that way

///

now they didn't dig they were into
headstones in the main they had an idea of a house
made entirely of headstones
for a window for a look outside one could feel a gone name
so it was common after dark that
they wore the stones on their shoulders towards the truck like
a ages ago bird wears out time above the stocks
where the rotten eyes of the robber gleam
and slop buckets of shit get brung
all the night by wiry kids learning early
all the wrong things what a shock justice suck a rotten egg
the evil green eye of a potato shaved
and riding at the back of the throat

///

carried like a cross the headstones
across their shoulders
and their knees wished they'd had mouths
fell down dented the earth   oh that a knee to graze could
and the powerful weight of a stoned name   cud
as they'd tried the inchworm shuffle
their chins soon too sunk in green mossy turf

///

but they were strong and they were stalwarts and they were in the wrong
in the main and dawn was coming you could tell it by
first frosted birds unwaxed hair ping at not dark
and the lines they made with their plowing chins were like lightning's
tracings wandering balance beaming tree root smoldering boom
boom

///

or they were two polar bears
silent as in an all day snow lisping in the enveloping nightsnow
white white on
unsuspecting explorer people dining

on astronaut snacks
inside the one polar bear a mouth
so cleansed of word as to be beautiful flesh garter
inside the other arm and hand
inside the hand compass churched clutched
inside the compass needle
inside the needle north? nothing
north is a feeling
only the underwear washwater knows
o the water as it falls against water having been wrung
is a little like a statue a shit bird beard a poop drool
and the ditches nigh a man and a half wide
and the half being the so called dreams he holds on to
or lets go like a blue tarp not tied down good enough

///

tell me do you have a blue blue tarp there down under yr underclothes
and do you count on the so many humans moving around
to ambient the crinkle of yr blue tarp out of this world

///

never you mind butttt can you believe of a day what an ear endures
being a nonselective gappy whorl
being a passive trap and conscienceless gorger
tell you it's like a cartoon lake a dream is jumping up off of you
or the wind won't not let you broadcast
cavity springfed subterranean dishtight diprap epithalamion
dead deer dreams dead cats crash creams bobcats dead
flapped and dangled sat perfect still
like a paper bone unwritten of wrath
wheel is a wheel
a wheel hath no valorous nose
machinewon worn ditches
rain'll top a road turn it hissing dish

///

these countryside men
taking none of the guff nor the care of carving
designs in their face hair
the parts
made in the kids' moptops according
to the currents of the river
cowlick that's a big spit
fish turtle fear flattening

///

now and then again some crazy man
dead wolf over the shoulder
every mouth a wound
diet of flour syrup butter and brandy
and the men's eyes
translated wilder maybe when they slept
wolves mated with their eyes
maybe they'd gone so wrong their eyes'd come fresh

///

maybe after a little longer their skulls to crack open
and a mess of wolves would spill out
to romp and playbite and lick and

///

woe unto you if yr gut pile shades out yr shit pile and
woe unto you if in reality you are the cause of yr
breakdowntime you are the breakdown time you yrself took
a look in the pissin silo nothin but wine took a peek
in the pissin toolbox pissin winecoolers brooked the
pissin shed pbr pbr like a rash they was always
visitin always steppin to town praise be to the river
too dirty to be the tincture to mend the true real life fracture all this is

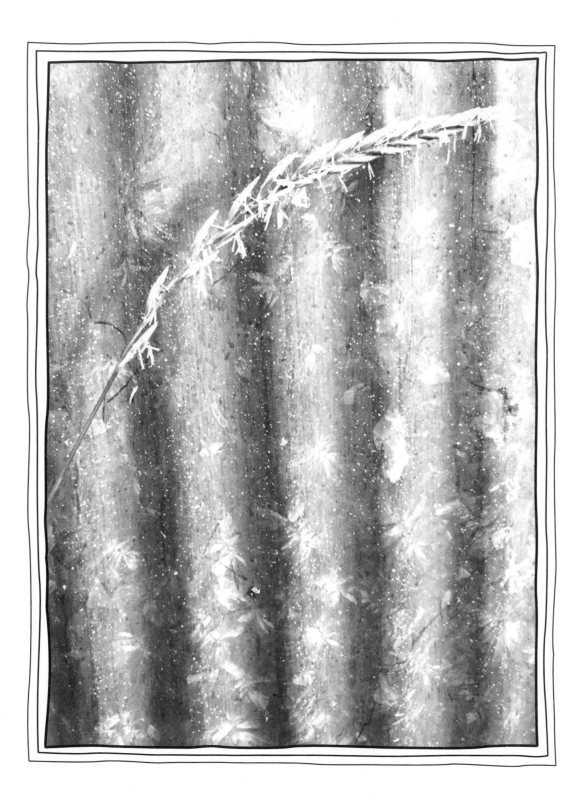

XI:
COUNTRY MUSIC

///

and this is riverwatersun
so generous pursy
belly flop of
on the bread sopped wine his eyes as he
lay fairly dreaming probably
least sleepy he'd ever been

///

in the garden
in the short shorts flesh like

///

to clean milk with glass

///

glass with milk

///

did a little local flip like somebody trying to die

///

trying to crawl in and burping contest with death

///

three four two are you ready to
swing
your eyes like a snowy hat swung hung clothes
closed?

///

as he ferret glugs his dick down his dick down
in into the close cropped ground least he was trying to
land a little unsure rest restless of him
but he relentless in an oaten grapple swing ing

///

swear it wasn't even really soft right there but he went ka da went on in
because flesh like glass walled washed with milk
with the bell-worms-in-the-ocelot move
in a sutra written on a hiway skin
talkin hots-in-the-hold
talkin baked potatoes
peekin their little green
eyes over the edge at that boil ten hundred bubble
syrup spit baked bean sea
it's alright if you look away

///

i am actually humming as done as children
to mate our outsound with the vacuum insound
back when the ceiling was the floor hanging upside down
i am actually doing the enervation karaoke thing

///

so we don't have to hear him groan
and grind and groan and grind and buckle and break
the trapdoor under the trapdoor under the trapdoor exploding
into the beheaded and drawn and quartered ligaments of the clover

///

an liquid thud ooom cult whom   an winged 4 3
and the zipper back up can't help it tends tent
and the dew buckets for the dews
on some one mysterious high
slow fill gain   kit
sun pull
to pull at and pulling
his eyes out of cross
mmmmmmoody dews
sssssassy trees
that's how this is

///

plus later one coyote
early under
one languid shucked moon
bulging hulky heroic over
the hairy boners of the hunted pines steps in
the wet gashed at and gunned in
is said to wear a shoe of manglass plain mason
coy in glassed footings

///

yes a walking toast cum jar to the moving moon oar
and hungry for
dig deep deep dig now
for the muscle in sat down water
for the onions opened house eyes

///

it's a pbr sponsored tractor no brakes keen nice footrot mastitis bluebag soremouth
yes just a little cantank in yr husbandry and you'll end be tractored out
and herniating it up at the fat sound factory before yr 30 up
at the debt hill wish an epic angel would shotput away now

a spider in the baa skull hole on the gut pile getting by
on exhausted shitty ass hoverers everybody's gotta eat

///

ain't it so
we are all crochetin one nimble trellis over
a zero sight hole and waiting
to grab gosh i hope knot unkink

///

unkink for the flow row

XII:
FINIS

///

tooth tooth heard he poop pooped and missed and
down they went into the dirty
misty watery flow i heard 2,309,402,398
worms accidentally nosed and bodied 'em
9/10th's a mile down from the last
dog's yard deuces heard they crawled by
the freeze and thaw by the heave and lift
and tumble by the dirt under is
its own ocean sort yr just not eye alive to that slow slow
truly there's nowhere's not a shore and bumpin long low low

///

and i heard they made the surface on
one unusual warm february day
a timing miracle each both as one up they came
as one and nigh and then 2 birds of a black oil
dump tint so either cat or cow birds not too
very gifted in sight
didn't see a house cat fart horse glue chew
elm or ash

///

and and   and an early bear slamming by
wreckless s-april s-april under and thru her
beary breath she means
like to eat a new fawn if may'd fall
into the bloomers of june say   poop spots say poop moon spew say pume

///

and a frost got on 'em duck on duck
did glint pretty plastic a picture of earrings
someone really pretty ice fishing with ice for fish

///

yes a trysty raring sun did all
through moss and limb to pike 'em look good comely

///

and friends are you still at me
i got rabbit blood in me vase my hare
along yr ear it's true it's soft and tickle it
a coyote what the helled it and it and
down the chomp by chunks maw mock
but nothing no nothing stays long in a wild dog straight race gut

///

and then mother of pearl another wild dog ate that scat
and then that wild dog ate a lost cat with a long
complicated string of names she was lost in
and then the two teeth lost of a bar bop
met up with the lost cat meat at a sock hop
it's 1950 according to the car show in the hardware parking lot
where wore out men guide their long guts around and
peering in at fine cloth and leather eyes
like cut fish and what would they
if those guts hatched
give a birth to
a 24 hr all you can eat sign throbbing
a blood sign
off the road side
before ya git ta town
pack 'er in and fart on home is
shit for brains glue hart

///

and i can say the teeth got
kept cozy cabin woodstove warm in the cat guts
and i can meow like a chipmunk in a cartoon
and elmer fudd shit the bed and the family farm shit the kayak
and you know i am soft kind gentle and
you know i am raised by women during
foreign wars whose strangers to kindness
are as the rain flipped
as a coin of cloth

///

from on high high how many sides has a drop? rob a leaf
for seat of pant go only dance i know is aquarium octopus
so you know so soft you could bite clean
through me and my bones

///

can't classical this the two teeth ain't
enshrined on a turd the cat guts didn't rust flesh to flesh
to improve energy on the run try cat up yr ferrous yap

///

love love happy happy cry crimelessness ho 2 tooth alive again
most excellent vibrancies alive in the whites
of trilliums alive in those lipsticked tissues clean through the darkest
parts of woods must have flirted from a church purse
on a open window car ride alive again in daisies in the 27 petal

shootin out the sides yes a raise of denticulate milks out the hazy beatific Z day0
and down in those ditches rubbin on nine minus 8 indian paint brushes
with some clever clover rubbin on some doily poison ivy under
with some worms rubbin on the roots of all that
with some stones down some lower doin steady eddy risin
the gall of the glacier the commandments of slush
the glacier a blind sculptor sculpts with his mouth

///

gray-son boo-keep cam-keel

///

was a time younger silo an 80footer and climbin it
the lightning bugs for toes and the pants
of wild dogs for heel strike up top now that was close
to flying and you could see the lights of the little town
when each one had a meaning and a feeling a person went-ing inside
to check on something a roast a sick kid
for there was no such thing as one checkered need up that
the breeze doin what breezes it freshed and then it slackened
it twisted a vine on a vine a no thing
up at air ware verse ground earth dirt herk
germanmerciless farmer you were young and jobbin for
strongest drink he ever took his own saliva
cleared throat to quench thirst

///

and you were young so a climber to tip the
deathtrap gasbelch silo topdoor shut
as tho one stylite of old but you were young so you did tip it
young and quick to yr purpose
yes the star light broad and thin as a qtip to tip a dirty ear to
and starting down rung now went ting-ting ling-ling the rivets
singing a little the rivets in the steel hoops abound the stays
and what is it binds the gird on a star? echo of a glass in sand moat pond souvenir

///

and the stones some steady rising
awkward glacier bang memory mad stone steel cad stone some disk ragging thumb chattel

///

until it got to where you almost did not want to
find the bottom rung the earth again the stones on the rise
a foot on it invitation to enter
and do it all again tomorrow
but you was young so

chafing at it all a little ah a little foam lit the night from yr mouth to see by to
stay up here a time to hesitate to pretend
what frothclocked thru yr guts wads not of earth
everything below you then
weighed down by its living self
only stones only steady rising and
the water enough hangin from bone enough to stay you

///

o to be you
air star eater for a second ah a truthful two three
to fill to the hilt with rag age both hi and low
yes to piss the light to shit the light to eye light to ear light to do a little hair lie array
and sew a bunch of seedsacks together so as not
to freak every tom and terry with an i out
and the feedsacks smoldering up
and the people coming running out
it is pitiful the way the people run
if you ever do a lick of work you will know it
cook a story it is beautiful
unpaid for trickster kale
upon his honest transcend dent self

///

cleared throat dirt scuffed gout crowling

///

this must be the ground or close

///

pray for rain pal pray against rain bale
may frog slurp back up at swamp tea shed
may the clover dense o dry o
squirm the bales together o dress 'em in a decent go at round ah
shittin coyote eats the field's mouse so to the mouse grey gets bound
waaaa the tractor sound
eats i can only tell you what i recall having heard someone saw

///

and this coytoe asnooze upon a ballyhoo bale bale
when the natural lights go out
be coy import when lights go bein that can of sweet grass if you
tender mouse die jest and waaa
to watch the insides of her wolfy eyelids awhile where well have i been counting
bales plus milk wound rabbits nursing
a 2 tooth

///

my people are so negative
the big fun it is tomorrow probably now
to be born under the wet chicken sun wet
whose leery eye catches at something
a potato a cream a crimination
a milk wound of
grassfat on mist field as tho
a pillowcase a wino as tho a buckhorn
a yellow streak as tho a back a beak
a snowed in car a shack a heat
a baby and a baby and a baby
and a baby and a baby and a baby
and a baby and a baby and a baby
and a baby was once one short squat

///

steam engine threadin train
the stump town to the thump town to the little liar city
to the people didn't eat wild animal only

///

if i am what i tongue and tooth and roof
let it be the wind thru them clingy pine bare assed and 20
and chasin bed round o we tipped on in
under quilts made by human hands what i mean
you could recognize what yr people worked in in it so
to crawl under felt pretty personal almost too much
blink hard swallows grandpa out of one time he bent
wrong and rrrrrip

///

one kerosene lamp there beside purrin
in that teapot of a shack what i mean it had
a lean to it because the builder had a crook in
his neck that day homebody bodyhome

///

and to tell it true
that first night we couldn't even you know she'd set
out traps she'd immediately recognized the infestation
those were no traveling rabbits leaving oval purchase
on their wavey way yes she set out 33 in total and every time
i'd lean in say her name make my voice husky but soft
like something washed 1000 times hung out wrung out beat dry
there one would pop off snap snnnap and there she'd be leaping

like sweet sweet wash water tossed
from the bed to drop another in the bucket she'd set
there by the door by dawn 27 traps shut the lives
of 27 mice making merry i can still feel us jump
when they snapped i can still feel the bed lift as she leapt
i can still hear the report of the springs i think i made
a stupid joke about the bedsprings were wore out old traps
and i'd cau- snap off went again can still hear her
prying the traps open the little grey yawn the trap made
being opened off a body i can still hear the mice bodies
and one rat fall in the bucket the sound of body against body
something like wallets picked off dead soldiers
dropped on rockpiles laced in snakes by birds the color of a hole drilled in ice

///

and did i haul 'em to the woods edge i did and did i look at them
as they rolled in a massy tumble like played out rags one helluva
spill it was like if smoke had some meat on it
it was nothing to me then you would hustle around and stay only
remotely acquainted with stillness

///

in the still wool quiet of that second night it was like a
tree in march young love spigot each other
river in ever tree never sleeps the world
is sure some washy unrest just waitin on a tap when i remember
that night i say it was like walking into a field after
the dark and you are killing sweet into yr nose's life as you go
the sweet of the clover the sweet of the strawberry
the purple the white the green the red and half the hay
is yours for the taking and that means something about how you'll
grow her she you and the light purple and white and red give
could be called old and new wounds or it couldn't
the mouth busy other ways always then

///

rainy loomy yes
of a headed sugar tomorrow tomato
and how did he rise   yes by the bullfrogs their catch of bucket water voices
and how did she rise   yes by the eyepatch wheel wool pitch of three crow
by they unfrenzied balking hold   but friendlylike as tho to spar with the hay
day done for fun what i mean there was no meanness to it
boys will bruise boys will be boys cowlick like a barnswallow nest
that's an awful sweet piece of metal yr sky-and-draggin

///

her one foot steppin down
her one foot grew a second nose on him
ah delicious quicksand try mild meat on fire
touched down ah a small smell smart
sprint 9 thou white pigeon freak talcum
as often from the horn of the young   to this day

///

and reaching to grasp at and grasping
to quake quite his tree
for a second rain shock to pep qualm say
a tree a living bank to rain say a living tomb to fall
say storm womb room say she walks is one
thing lou yaa you need not oval yr mock maw to bray

///

his chewing done
by her heel-in-palm
-and-up-through-the-windows hands

///

walks his lore meat on

///

walks his on

///

walks his

///

a dandy to a doings
a randy damn dandy
to the limit one time

///

nothin's perfect price it's high

///

honey honey can you hear them bells
tollin that's us hammering to get a thing
to be the thing gonna
trial it
its in fits
til it fits

///

be through by dark
at least until the dew
lays in sets in

///
wend that belt through
wrestle it on now
bleed that line

///
to tally time to breakdown
time to fuse 'em as in
a cattail a microphone as in
a thousand next year cattail song the promise of
the breaded spines of
uprightness of stockstillness

///
sing sail

///
sail into it
skim it shave it
scoop it coop it
dock it band it

///
gonna feed that out
gotta wean that off
that's a song the people hear
could be 33 miles if
the wind is right

///
the bellow o' desperation separation love
honestly the cops have come

///
sing

///
haul it
spread it shim it rig it ring it
shim it to
the limit

///
a time
one time
once upon a field
his field
his times

///

hawk and sun
horsefly deerfly
with a little sick
bloodface obsession

///

hawking sun
lock and key
wide door
wild door
wilder
wider

///

now thrush that edge numb now

///

be there
bare there
he'll be there
bare and bared and
new to young

ACKNOWLEDGMENT

Deepest gratitude to the editors of the following journals, where snippets of this book first appeared: *Entropy Magazine*; *Third Coast*; *TAMMY*; *Diagram*; *Academy of American Poets*, *Poem-A-Day*; *Colorado Review*; *Gulf Coast*; *jubilat*; *Small Fires Press*; *Fanzine*; and *Burnside Review*.

THANKS

Through whom, in whom:

Doris Pfalzgraf, Monica Detra, William Harold Detra, Linda Detra, Richard Smith, Pam Carazo, Patrick Kavanagh, Meggan Meisegeier, Erin Kavanagh, Angus Meisegeier, Rosy Meisegeier, Pippin Meisegeier, Emily Wittman, Joel Brouwer, Ashley Chambers, Steve Timm, Jason Busse, Joshua Marie Wilkinson, Rodney Smith-Wittman, Heidi Lynn Staples, Eric Parker, John Staples, Nathan Parker, Shobha Rao, Scott McWaters, Dave Marr, Kate Bernheimer, Jeanie Thompson, Scott Hunter, Joyelle McSweeney, Johannes Goransson, Ashley McWaters, Craig Pickering, Mark Ehling, Shelly Taylor, Greg Brownderville, Patty Wheeler, Ander Monson, Stephen McClurg, John Wingard, John Pursley III, Stephanie Ray, Molly Dowd, Billy Sedlmayr, Anna McConnell, John Miller, Sandra Simonds, Jenny Gropp, David Floyd, Sarah Blackman, Carol Eichelberger, Jean Mills, Wendy Rawlings, Aubrey Lenahan, Marsha McSpadden, Warner Moore, Tim Earley, KC Vick, Beth Harrison, Ed Zeizel, Kristen Schiele, Susan Brennan, Jane Detra, Bob Davenport, Joy Detra, Tim Croft, Eva Schultz, Sonya Pritzker, Jim Schultz, Shrode Hargis, Patti White, and Jerry Goldberg.

In the realm of the can't thanks enough – there's the TMR/TMB crew: Chet, Ben, Kim, and Tristan.

Photo by Robert Smith